The Simplicity of Herbal Health

Oakwell Classes

by

Phyllis Heitkamp Master Herbalist

authorHOUSE

1663 LIBERTY DRIVE, SUITE 200
BLOOMINGTON, INDIANA 47403
(800) 839-8640
www.authorhouse.com

© 2004 Phyllis Heitkamp Master Herbalist.
All Rights Reserved.

Cover photograph by Steven Foster
Copyright 2004 Steven Foster

No part of this book may be reproduced, stored in a retrieval system, or transmitted by any means without the written permission of the author.

First published by AuthorHouse 06/29/04

ISBN: 1-4184-2250-9 (sc)

Printed in the United States of America
Bloomington, Indiana

This book is printed on acid-free paper.

Disclaimer

This book was written to help you make informed decisions. We need to be a part of the decision-making process in regard to our health. As you learn what is available, you can assist your health care provider and take responsibility for your part. Always find a health care provider that encompasses your philosophy of health and work together. It is your body and you need to make the final decision but this is impossible unless you find all of your options. This book is just one of many options that you have, find as many as you can before you make your "informed" decision.

Dedication

This book was written for my students: past, present and future as I feel all people should have some basic knowledge of how to help themselves even if it is just being more informed as to what is available. My students have pushed me to write this book so they can share this information with others.

My children, Kathy, Blaine and Loren Grayson helped me promote my last book, Wisconsin Medicinal Herb. They told me that they were very proud of that book. They felt it was well done so they encouraged the writing of this one.

The format comes as a request from my sister, Donna Lemke, who asked me to keep it simple so anyone can understand how to use herbs without needing to study in depth. My California sister, Betty Westphal, has always been able to move me forward on those days when things bogged down so I was able to complete this work.

None of this would have happened if my husband, LaVern Heitkamp, hadn't given me the time and space to do this. It has taken him a while to come around to herbs but he will ask if I have something for whatever the situation is and then report back on how it worked, sometimes to his surprise.

Making everything readable was the job of my wonderful and patient aunt, Catherine Harris. Reading everything for its grammar and punctuation is a lot different than for content but she is good at that.

My friend Linda Pavlovich, a surgical nurse, helped me keep all the body parts in the right places and helping me understand how they worked.

I wish to thank all my friends who have been very understanding when I have been too busy or unavailable.

Most of all, I need to thank my teachers and mentors for changing my life in this manner, for helping me find my "mission."

Introduction to Herbs

Sometimes I get too excited about herbs and herbal health. I want to run out and give everyone a book so they have information on this stuff. I can't think of one home that doesn't need to know something about herbs.

Then I remember what Dr. John R. Christopher always said, "Don't run until you are called." Some people just aren't ready for this knowledge. It sure is hard to remember this as I bite my lip when someone is telling me about all the medications they are on or all the surgery that they have had done. I try to remember that perhaps they needed that to learn from or to get attention with?

It is a planet of choice and because you are reading this, my guess is that you are ready to choose an organic way to help your body heal and stay healthy.

The main question is why study Herbal Health?

There are many reasons; one of them may be that people are looking for answers to physical problems that they are not getting assistance with from the medical community. More and more people are not willing to put up with the reactions that are coming from chemicals created in a laboratory. Many people are finding that the original problem is gone only to find a different one in its place.

Others get involved with herbs because we live in a "temporary" world. They have become part of the permanent/part-time employees, having no insurance coverage. They found that herbs are inexpensive compared to the chemical compounds found in drug stores after the expense of a doctor's appointment.

Most of the time the needed herbs are growing in our backyards, but now what to do with them, how do we use them. I want to teach how to make a capsule, salve, tincture, ointment, suppository, infusion, decoction, and tonic. Show how to know the difference between a fomentation and a poultice. Then I want to show how to use these different preparations to assist the body in healing itself.

Still other people want to have more control over their bodies and their health, wishing not to put inorganic chemicals into an organic body. They are nursing their babies to stay away from baby formulas with chemicals added. They are home-schooling their children with results that rival national honors. They are making their own soap to keep chemicals out of their homes, or making their own baby food so they know what goes into it. They are growing free-range chickens to keep hormones out of their food supply. They have gardens or subscribe to organic farms even though it may be a little more expensive because they don't want the sprays and chemical fertilizers in their food supply.

No, I am not talking about the "hippies" of the '60's but a new movement that is taking place all over the world. There are more and more of us and this movement is growing faster than the business world is at the present time. Little by little we are becoming educated as to what we have done or are doing on this planet. I feel that people are ready to take responsibility more than ever before. We are an "underground" movement.

We have been trained to "Let someone else" be responsible for everything from what we eat, to making us happy or well. Most people believe that the medical profession can give them a quick fix. It seems that the side effects of the chemicals are what other people experience and not us. It isn't until we are hit with either a major side effect or we aren't getting any effect at all including the healing of our body, that we decide to look at another healing modality. (There are many ways to heal and herbs is just one of the many.)

Most people come to this study with an agenda. It could be to help a family member who isn't getting well, or a very personal problem that the inorganic chemicals are not handling or have created more problems than they have solved.

I have been teaching these classes for 10 years, so my students have directed the creation of this book with their questions and interests. It is the student that didn't show any interest in class, who calls me six months or even a year later to ask a question, or the animated student who wants to know if I give advanced classes or where they can learn more, that have asked me to create this book. They tell me that they have friends who would like to take my classes but live too far away. They think that a book that would teach what they have learned would be great. So for them, I write this book.

While lectured all over the State of Wisconsin, I have found people hungry for the "How to" of herbs. That with a little bit of oil and wax, along with the plants that grow in their apple orchard, they can make a salve for their cow, horse, dog or even the baby with the skin rash. This would cost them less than one-tenth of an appointment to a chemical practitioner.

No, I am not an herbal practitioner who treats people with herbs but I do teach them both what would be helpful and how to use it. That is what this book is all about. There are hundreds of herb books that tell us what to use for what situation, but they don't teach us how to do it. I decided that unless we know how to use the plants from the back yard, there is no need to learn about what herb does the job.

My teachers; Hanna Kroeger of Colorado; David and Fawn Christopher of the School of Natural Healing, in Utah; and Dr. James Duke of Maryland; the first one only taught the "What" to use for what problem but the last three gave me the "How and Why" of herbs.

As you read this book, you will see the "How and Why" is in every chapter. I explain in a step by step process, how to make Infusions, Decoctions, Tonics, Tinctures, Salves and more.

I have presented 60 herbs, talking about what they are capable of doing and how to use them and in a lot of cases how they work on the body. This book talks about body parts and some problems each area might encounter. I have included information that was given to me about these areas from my teachers along with specific area information from other authors.

I do need to explain one term that you will encounter in this text and that is *vibrational.*

When I went to study with Hanna Kroeger, she seemed to have a lot of alternative answers to many health problems. Hanna would explain what to use for what. She had created many herbal formulas as well as "*Vibrationals*". Her *Vibrationals* are based on the electro-magnetic energy of whatever they are to be used for. As an example: Shingles is found to vibrate at a minus some-vibration, so Hanna produced a product that contained the plus of that vibration. (The equipment to measure this is not lawful in the USA but is used extensively in Europe.)

The difference between *Vibrational*s and homeopathics is that there is no Shingles Virus used to make the *Vibrational* so one is not putting Shingles into the body. The premise of homeopathics is that "like handles like." So they put a bit of Shingles Virus into the solution and dilute it hundreds of times to make their remedy. With Vibrationals one is negating the vibration of the problem and allowing the body to flush it out.

After studying with Hanna for a while, I came away feeling that maybe there is hope on this planet. I hadn't found it in the medical community.

I wanted more information than I got from Hanna Kroeger. I wanted to know how herbs worked. My next step was to find an herbal school. As I checked out this one and that one, I learned that Dr. John R. Christopher with his School of Natural Healing had trained the founders of most of the present day herb schools.

The program at the School of Natural Healing was all that I expected and more. At first I remember telling my daughter that it was so foreign to what we have been taught, that I was having difficulty with it. She reminded me that I only had to agree with them until I got my degree. Now I can't think in any other way to do healing because it makes more and more sense. I guess that is why it is called "Natural" healing.

When life is great and we travel in "Same old, same old" patterns, we don't explore new things. It takes a crisis to shift our perspective. Because you are reading this material, you are ready to do the shift and start taking more responsibility for your health, and the health of those around you.

May this book just be a start to an exciting, healthy adventure.

Table of Contents

Chapter I 1
   Tea time 1
   A New Way of Thinking 4
   Zone I 10
   Zone II. 14
   This brings us to Zone III 19
   Where To Start 25
   Chapter 1 - Resources 30

Chapter II 31
   Tea time 31
   The Liver 33
   The Lymph System 43
   Making a Decoction 46
   Blood Cleansers 48
   Eyes and Ears 58
   Where Do We Start? 63
   Chapter II - Resources 64

Chapter III 66
   Tea of the Day 66
   The Heart 67
   Making a Tonic 70
   Sugars 76
   High Blood Pressure 80
   Herbs for the Brain 84
   What is a Nervine? 90
   Chapter III - Resources 96

Chapter IV **97**
    Dandelion Wine 97
    Harvesting and Storing 99
    Making A Tincture 109
    Herb Walk 115
    Standardization 132
    Chapter IV - Resources 133

Chapter V **135**
    Another Wonderful Tea 135
    Kidneys 137
    Our Skin 144
    Making A Skin Salve 151
    Sexual Health 159
    Chapter V - Resources 170

Chapter VI **171**
    Tea Time 171
    The Pancreas 172
    Hanna's Miscellaneous Notes 187
    Hanna's Workbook 191
    Other Healing Modalities 195
    Herbal Health 200
    Chapter VI – Resources 202

Chapter I
Tea time

We're going to start this study with a tea. A peppermint tea would be nice. Peppermint is easy to grow in a garden or in a flowerpot so you have some fresh all the time, but if you don't have fresh, even the tea bags are nice.

When we make a medicinal tea, we put a teaspoonful of cut-up herb (plant) into a teacup, then pour hot distilled water over the herb of choice. We cover the cup with a lid or even the saucer as not to lose the volatile oils, they are a part of the healing process, (Aromatherapy) then let it steep for 5 minutes.

See, herbal healing isn't so hard, you have already made your first preparation and it is called an infusion.

In an infusion, we infuse distilled water with the constituents of the plant material. This is the reason that we use distilled water, because it is "hungry" water. For all practical purposes, there is nothing but Hydrogen and Oxygen in distilled water. We know that this isn't entirely so, as it comes from plastic bottles out of stainless steel distillers. Basically it is void of most contaminants so it welcomes the carotene, the chromium, the niacin, the phosphorus, the potassium and even the tannins along with all other things that are present in this wonderful Peppermint herb.

This is why a simple tea is so healing. It is giving up these ingredients so that you can nourish your body with them.

You have just started to become an herbalist. Congratulations!

* * *

As this is an herbal study, let's learn about our first herb, Peppermint.

As a member of the mint family, it has some of the same characteristics that all mints have. One is the square stem. Another is the opposite leaves. The flowers form circles at the top of the plant. There are many members of the mint family and they all tend to be somewhat aromatic.

That means they give off a smell but believe me, they don't all smell great like peppermint. Some members of this family include Catnip, Lavender, Oregano, Marjoram, Thyme, Sage, Basil, Motherwort, Bergamot, and Hyssop. As you can see it is a very large family and we haven't named all of them here.

They are easy to grow and propagate in a small garden but they do tend to get out of hand if not watched so a good gardener sets limits as to how much space they can take up or where they can grow.

Peppermint is a very popular herb being used in many day-to-day products from soaps to toothpaste but what do we really know about it?

One of the first things we will learn is that Peppermint has the ability to kill germs. According to Dr. Varro Tyler it is the menthol oils that are the active ingredient to do this. Having just checked Dr. James Duke's database, I find that there are about 240 ingredients in Peppermint. Then I found that 70 of these active ingredients are found in the leaves while only about 20 are found in the essential oils of this plant. So it seems that eating the leaves or using them in a tea might give us access to more of these ingredients.

What do all of these ingredients or constituents do? They have the ability to calm the stomach and upper gastrointestinal tract. This would include things like colic, nausea, hiccoughs, indigestion, stomachache, and gas, along with vomiting. Because it has such a mild taste, even children will drink a cup of Peppermint tea.

Peppermint will also help with major problems. It can help with gallstones, with fevers and headaches, with diarrhea and intestinal flora abnormalities. It has been used successfully for laryngitis, and toothache along with earaches and bronchitis.

It is even heavy duty, as it also has properties that are helpful against cancers and tumors.

How can it do all of this? It is giving the body a smorgasbord of ingredients with which to cleanse and rebuild. We will be going into how herbs work and we will find out that by getting the toxins out and the nutrition in, the body has the ability to rebuild.

The Simplicity of Herbal Health

While listening to a friend teach about essential oils, I heard her talk about Peppermint oil being "of the highest vibration." She talked about getting well by raising your vibration and that low vibrations support illnesses. You have noticed this. When you are upset about something or have had a large loss in your life, you are more liable to get a cold than when things are going well in your life.

Because Peppermint has this very high vibration in it, Hanna has stated that when anyone is using one of her vibrational remedies, Peppermint must be avoided, as it will interfere with the ability of the vibrational remedies to work. (See definition of vibrational remedies in the introduction.)

Dr. Christopher suggested that when you have a cold or flu, a cup of Peppermint tea would be helpful, as it is a stimulator for the body. This means that it activates the systems to fight colds or the flu. When we stimulate the body, it goes to work for us.

My daughter Kathy called me from her home one hundred miles away and told me that she had been sick for a week. Because we don't go to the doctor for every little thing, she was running out of vacation days at work and didn't know what to do. I packed a bag and drove up to her home. The first thing that I did was to make some Peppermint tea. Then I had to decide what herbs would handle the present problem. By the next morning she was up and around and feeling fine. Herbs really do work.

As an additional note: My wonderful teacher, Rev. Hanna Kroeger said that placing a sprig of fresh Peppermint on the picture of a person undergoing surgery, will help them heal faster.

Whenever my husband smells Peppermint he is reminded of the time we took a tour at Celestial Seasonings in Boulder, Colorado. At this tea manufacture's factory, they have a separate room in which they keep the Peppermint. All the other flavors are in the main warehouse but Peppermint is kept separate because they said that it was too strong and would adulterate the other herbs. When one walks into the Peppermint room, one can only stay a short time as the wonderful smell is overpowering. Perhaps it is this energy that Hanna was using when she suggested that a sprig of Peppermint on a picture would help them to heal faster?

Phyllis Heitkamp Master Herbalist

A New Way of Thinking

In the course of this study we will be talking about a new way of thinking regarding dis-ease. I call this dis-ease because the body is not comfortable, it is not happy and in balance. We know that the world is full of germs so we need to find out how to live here with them. In this book, we are going to find out how to get well and how to stay well.

We were born with a perfect vehicle to house our spirit in a third dimensional world. We are not this body but we need it to do the things that we want to do here. Did you know that our bodies are designed to function for hundreds of years? Dr. Deepac Chopra mentioned that we are designed to rebuild our parts as they wear out and he even mentioned that we are doing that at a faster rate than we have ever done it before. Years ago it was said that we rebuild our organs every 7 years. This meant that all the cells of each organ were new every seven years. Dr. Chopra mentioned in his lecture that we are now replacing our organs in months instead of years. He also said that there are reasons that we are not duplicating them perfectly. The reasons being, the chemicals that we breathe, eat and live with, such as pollution and pesticides along with all the food additives.

In the book, <u>The Elves Of Lily Hill Farm</u>, by Penny Kelly, we are told why we are not staying healthy. She says, "Where our ancestors used to eat a huge variety of some three hundred food items as part of their annual diet, the average American diet now included only a handful of foods which we eat over and over again. No wonder overwhelming allergies are among the fastest-growing health complaints! Not only is the body subjected to the same foods every week, we aren't getting the benefit of the nutrients contained in the foods we aren't eating." In another part of this book Kelly says, "As the fine root hairs of growing plants worked their way through this kind of soil, (She is talking about live soil, no chemicals and loaded with micro-organisms) they wrapped themselves tightly around the individual crumbs. Once the crumb was firmly in their grasp, they emitted a variety of humic acids. These plant-emitted acids combined with the gooey excretions of the bacteria and micro-organisms living in the soil...all of which reacted chemically with nutrients and trace minerals trapped in the soil crumb around which the root was wrapped. These acids helped break the soil crumb into its basic elements making them available for absorption by the plants."

The Simplicity of Herbal Health

So in healthy soil we have all the trace minerals and microorganisms, but present-day farmers put only three things on their fields over and over. They are put on as a petroleum fertilizer from one of the chemical companies.

Herbs are, for the most part, weeds and they really don't care what the farmer or anyone does with the top two feet of soil. Some herbs like Alfalfa will put roots down as deep as 20 to 30 feet. How about trees like Oak? We use the bark of the Oak for healing. Oak roots might go down more than 100 feet and if it needs something to stay healthy, it just puts new hair roots out and finds what it needs. When we are supplementing our diet with herbs we are adding the nutrients that will help us go the extra distance.

I like to tell my classes that had I designed these bodies, I would have left out all sorts of things that keep us in balance. Take the skin for example, it creates a barrier on the outside of our body and on the inside. We are hematically sealed. This means that our blood supply is secured from outside invaders. To compliment this, we have friendly bacteria that live on the outside of our bodies to eat anything that comes to that area that doesn't belong there.

On the inside we have a mucus membrane covering the skin. This mucus is in contact with air, food, and water. In this mucus membrane, we have macrophages, (they look like golf balls with the dimples coming out and they act like Pac-man) they gobble up any pollution, chemicals and germs that come into the body.

I find this information fascinating because in order to understand how herbs work we need to understand a simplified version of how the body works.

Did you know that there are four ways for toxins to get out of the body? These are the lungs, the skin, the bladder and the bowels. We will be talking about how to help these organs as we learn more about herbs.

Unlike a car, we are self-healing. We can rebuild if 10% of what we want to heal is healthy, but we need to assist the body in doing this and now we are ready to find out how.

* * *

Phyllis Heitkamp Master Herbalist

How do we assist the rebuilding of our bodies? What do we need? We need food, water and air.

First, let's talk about food. What kind of food rebuilds bodies? Fruits, Vegetables, Whole Grains, Nuts and Seeds are mucusless foods. Well, that is what Dr. Christopher of the School of Natural Healing called them. They don't overload the system with a lot of mucus as some foods tend to do.

We need to eat foods raw but we can't eat enough of them that way. Raw foods haven't lost any of the enzymes or vitamins that cooked foods lose. So to get these enzymes, we need to eat some raw food daily.

Did you notice that I wrote WHOLE GRAINS? That is because when we eat grains that have been crushed, as in flakes, the life force has been taken out of the grain. When grain is crushed, it does not have the vitality that it had in its whole state. It has been killed or oxidized. The life force is gone. You can plant a whole grain and it will sprout but when you plant corn flakes or oatmeal, nothing will grow. It is important to put life into our bodies.

I tell my students how to make a great breakfast out of whole grains. First, one puts oat grouts (or any whole grain such as wheat berries or millet) into a mug. I usually fill the container one-fourth of the way to the top with the grain of choice. Then I add a dried fruit; raisins, dried prunes or apricot and pour hot water over everything until the hot water comes up to the top of the container. This stands covered over night and in the morning I have a great, filling breakfast.

I had a student call to ask how to make oat milk or grain milk and I think I would make it the same way as I have just described for my breakfast. I would soak the whole grain in hot water over night and strain off the mineral and vitamin-rich water in the morning.

Did you know that soaked or sprouted grains are better for the body than crushed or dried because soaking changes the pH? The grain goes from an acid food to an alkaline food and is therefore more digestible.

* * *

The Simplicity of Herbal Health

Penny Kelly states that in the twenties and thirties the idea was to have big farms that would feed the world. This was called agri-business. The farmers put in huge crops and used chemical fertilizers to make sure that the plants were fed. They used chemical pesticides and herbicides to control the bugs and weeds. Little did they know that this would also kill the soil. She states that, " the first generation of people raised on dead or deficient foods...suffered serious cavities, dental abscesses and total loss of teeth at an early age. But we covered these symptoms with fluoride." (Another poison)

She goes on to say, " The next generation of people raised with serious nutritional deficiencies in the forties and fifties had experienced a subtle worsening of bone and organ structures." She lists, ear, nose and throat problems along with tonsillitis and appendicitis in epidemic proportions.

In the Sixties and Seventies, she sights teeth problems, bone deformities and poor immune systems along with overwhelming allergies to the elements in nature.

She lists the problems of the eighties and nineties, "... in addition to poor bone structure, low immune response, and mental/emotional problems, they were beginning to exhibit such things as congenital brain and central nervous system anomalies," along with childhood cancers, arthritis, killer allergies and asthma, learning problems and even the inability to bond and socialize in normal ways. "We were trying to cover these symptoms by blaming our genes...and expansion of the criminal justice systems as our next answer to the problems at hand...problems that were really nutritional at their heart."

From this we can understand that the fruits, vegetables, whole grains, nuts and seeds need to be non-toxic or organic to benefit us.

Did you know that fruits have vitamins, minerals and even protein? One (1) fig has 3.5 grams of protein. Did you know that vegetables have vitamins, minerals and protein? One (1) cup of broccoli has 36 grams of protein. Whole grains have vitamins, minerals and fiber! Nuts and Seeds are loaded with trace minerals and protein. Dr. John R. Christopher calls these five things, "The Mucusless Diet" because they will nourish the body without creating excessive mucus. When excessive mucus is formed in the body, the natural defense system is compromised. The macrophages are overwhelmed and have trouble keeping the system clean.

Phyllis Heitkamp Master Herbalist

* * *

Now let's look at the water needs of our bodies. According to Dr. F. Batmanghelidj, in his book <u>Your Body's Many Cries For Water</u>, when the body is thirsty, there is already cellular damage.

Did you know that the fat in your body is 20% water? That the blood is 80% water? That the bones are 25% water, the connective tissue is 60% and the liver is 70%, the lungs are 92%, the muscles are 75%, the kidneys are 80%, the skin is 70%, the brain gray matter is 85% and the brain's white matter is 75%. Our bodies demand water to function. We need 1 oz for every pound of body weight per day. This doesn't mean that we need to drink a gallon of water but we have to take in at least that much per day in some form of liquid. It can be juice, soup, some juicy vegetable like tomato or even a juicy peach. Anything that provides us with the liquid that will supply the water content to the body. Things like coffee and colas do not work as they remove more liquid than they put in. They are diuretics. Dr. Christopher talked about the 10 kinds of water in his book <u>Regenerative Diet</u>. He said that there is: hard water, boiled water, raw water, rain water, snow water, filtered water, soft water, de-ionized water, reverse osmosis water, and distilled water. He says that our bodies can only use the H_2O and not all the other things that come with most of the waters mentioned. So distilled water furnishes just what the body needs and nothing else.

Dr. Christopher suggests that for all the minerals that are needed, like calcium and iron, should come from plant matter. Plants are able to break these minerals down to cell size with the acid that Penny Kelly talked about. There is no area in our body where enough acid is made to break minerals down so that the body can utilize them.

I was talking to a lady today and she mentioned the amount of waste matter that is allowable in her local city water. Then as I was paging through a book and the author mentioned that he liked to drink from this farmer's well even though he knew that he was taking in 4 glasses of junk a year. That doesn't sound like much but it is that much more that the body has to process to keep us healthy.

The second best in kinds of water that Dr. Christopher suggested is reversed osmosis water as only the tiniest particles are able to get through the filter membrane.

* * *

The third thing that is needed to rebuild the body is fresh air. This means really getting the air into our lungs and deep breathing a couple of times a day. The best place to do this is in an area where there are plants, not while stuck on the freeway in heavy traffic. If you find that there is no place in your area where there are a lot of plants, creating a small jungle in your apartment or house, might be just what is needed. This might also be a place where you relax, meditate, or just plan/review your day.

Plants are so important to all of us. They could live very nicely on this planet without us but we can not survive for even one day without them. They are the lungs of this planet and contribute the oxygen for our survival. We will be talking more about other ways that plants help us in later chapters of this book. As for now, we need to use the benefits that they create...basically our breathable air. Not only do they give us oxygen but clean our air by recycling a lot of the pollution.

In regard to deep breathing, one must remember that we have a nose created to temper the air temperature as well as filter particles out while we breath. It is very important to breathe through the nose when we do this deep breathing.

When I am not feeling well, I find that deep breathing is just the ticket. It gets oxygen into the body fast. This is not something that one should do standing up as it can create a feeling of dizziness. As much as we have heard about antioxidants, we still need oxygen. A lot of maladies are handled by oxidation. This means that we have oxidized the cells.

* * *

Now that we know what we need to rebuild this body, let's find out how we do this. It all starts in the digestive system, so let's look at this area.

ZONE 1

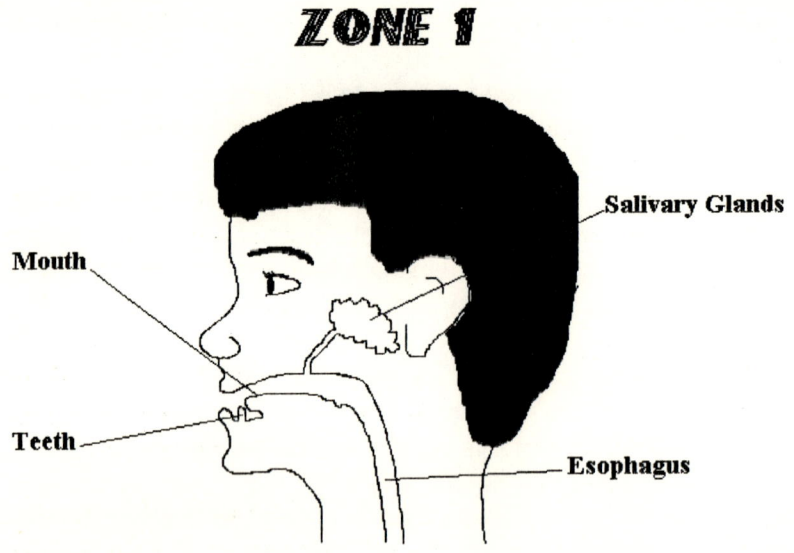

Zone I

The mouth is a very important area of the body in keeping us healthy. This is where we start digestion. It is the only part of the body that has grinders (Teeth). This is where all of our food is ground up so that digestion can take place.

This is where most people start creating their health problems. They chomp, chomp, swallow; never chopping the food into small enough particles or mixing the saliva into the food. It is the saliva that reduces bacteria by being in the alkaline range. The bacteria that aren't happy with this pH will be reduced.

It is also the only part of the body that can taste. Once a tasty morsel is swallowed, it can no longer be tasted. So then one has to have another piece to taste it and another and another. These taste morsels turn into pounds. If instead, one piece would be chewed and chewed, not only would the taste linger, but also the bacteria would be destroyed with the saliva mixed in and the stomach wouldn't have to do so much of the work because the particles would be smaller.

The Simplicity of Herbal Health

People, who have a loss of taste, lack zinc in their bodies. This can cause cellular damage as they also experience a lack of hydrochloric acid in the stomach according to Hanna Kroeger. Zinc is found in Oak, Spinach, Cucumber, Dill, Black Beans, Sassafras, Plums, Asparagus, Tomato, Cauliflower, Ginseng, Brussels sprouts, and nuts of all kinds.

Dr. Christopher had a saying, " Drink your food and chew your liquids." He meant that the saliva should be mixed not only with your solid food but liquid food as well. That juice needs to have the saliva mixed into it also before it is swallowed.

Rosemary Gladstar, speaker at HerbFest 2000, suggested that we should eat less and chew more. She was referring to attaining longevity and well being under the subject of "Recipes for Wellness."

Rev. Hanna Kroeger had a couple of tidbits of information dealing with the teeth. She suggested placing sliced Strawberries (the wild kind) on the teeth, to whiten the teeth. She also suggested cooking Red Raspberries down to a sauce (without sugar or water), then place this thick paste on the teeth for a short time, to remove all the plaque.

I have a personal problem with the teeth. As far as I know, no one had been able to rebuild teeth. Dr. Christopher did mention something about his toothpowder combination and how some people who had used it for a long time were having problems with filling popping out because the enamel was growing under the fillings but I have never known anyone to grow teeth.

We grow bone and teeth are an extension of bone but no one can tell us how to grow them. Instead they chip away at what we have. I work with stone and wood and plants. I can grow plants but not stone or wood and if I scratch on stone or wood, I lose some of the material. Yet our present system of tooth care asks for the scraping of our teeth to remove plaque. There has to be a better way to do this.

* * *

Out of all the herbs that assist Zone I, we will start with Oak Bark. Oak Bark is high in tannins so it is astringent. This is helpful in pulling things together and this makes oak bark good at tightening teeth. This astringent property is useful for many areas of the body that have lost their elasticity. I would like to try it on loose skin that comes from loosing weight and instead of Preparation H for tightening the skin in areas such as under the eyes. I can think of many uses for these tannins.

Oak Bark is also used to help with pyorrhea, a dis-ease of the gums. I make an Oak Bark tea to get more usable calcium in my body because Oak Bark is high in calcium along with all the other constituents that help the body utilize calcium quickly. Dr. Christopher suggested putting a strip of oak bark between our lip and gums and leave it there over night or even during the day. This would help the calcium content in the whole mouth area. Did you know that receding gums (Long in the tooth) isn't something that happens naturally as we get older? It is malnutrition of that area. This means that the gums are not getting proper nutrition. By putting Oak Bark in that area, all of its constituents can be utilized. Oak Bark having as many as 42 properties from Chromium to Zinc according to Globalherb's computer print-out. Globalherb states that the bark has 3.7% Calcium, which is a very high percentage for anything in the plant world.

* * *

Another herb that is a great healer in this area is Chaparral. I have used a tincture of this herb to clean up a tooth abscess in less than 6 hours. Chaparral is a great blood cleanser so it worked by putting the tincture next to the abscess in my cheek until it went down and the tooth could be worked on. The FDA tells us that Chaparral is dangerous but it has been used as a blood cleanser for a very long time. In fact, it is so good that it has been used to "clean up" some cancers.

* * *

Black Walnut tincture is another favorite of mine because of its high iodine content. It is the organic iodine that turns the green of the hull to black as it oxidizes. For a great many years iodine was used as a disinfectant. Well, it can still be used that way because it kills bacteria. By adding a little of it to the rinse water after brushing our teeth, we can kill any bacteria that are there and rinse them away.

When I am traveling, I like to add a dropper full to the local bottled water to reduce the bacteria count before drinking. We will be talking more about Black Walnut in later chapters.

*   *   *

Hanna suggests that the tongue is an extension of the intestine so for people with bad breath, she suggests that the person work on cleaning up the intestine, which we will be discussing later in this chapter or working on the health of the lungs. For the lungs, she has an herbal combination that includes garlic, Rosehips, Rosemary, Echinacea Root and Thyme. She calls this combination *Sound Breath*.

Another bit of information that Hanna talked about that applies to this area is the fact that when surgery is done and 10% of tonsils are left, they will grow back.

*   *   *

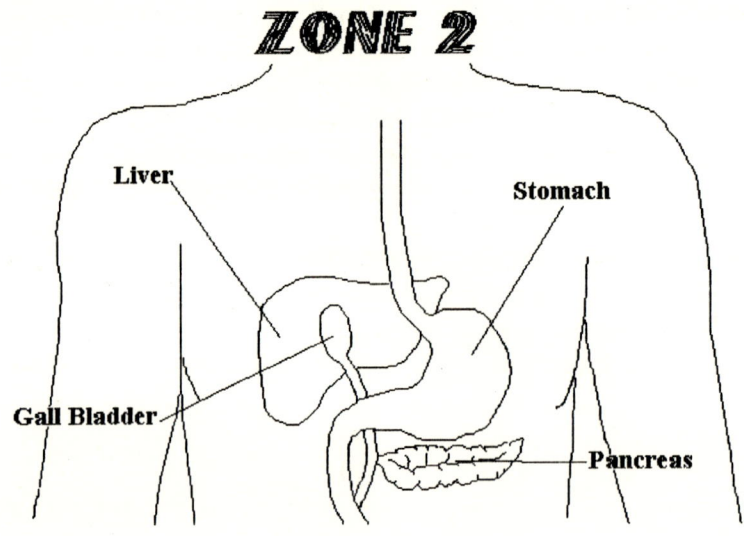

Zone II.

This zone is the stomach. It is here that more bacteria are gotten rid of, those not happy with an acid environment will be destroyed. Bacteria have a very narrow range of pH that they are happy in, so here is our second line of defense against dis-ease.

This acid environment is the natural condition of the stomach and here is where most of us get into trouble. People, with stomach ulcers caused by the germ Helicobacter pylori, have allowed the bacteria to get past Zone I and into an environment that they are very happy in. When we don't chew our food properly to insure that digestion has started in zone I, the stomach has to do all the work. The body has to increase the acidity to do all the digestion. After it has been doing this for 10-20 years, it stays at a very high acid content and the normal reaction then is to take an antacid tablet to counteract all the acid. This only makes it worse as the body, being very intelligent, just increases the acid to its normally high acid condition.

It is the lower portion of the stomach that makes the acid and after years and years of abuse, it just continues to make acid. Most of the time there is too much acid and a condition called acid reflux is evident. This is when

The Simplicity of Herbal Health

the stomach acid is overly abundant and comes up the esophagus. Again, anti-acids make this so much worse. Sometimes as people get older, they find that it has been overly abused to the point where there isn't enough hydrochloric acid left to digest their food.

I have found that a tablespoon of Apple Cider Vinegar in a glass of water will return the stomach to its rightful condition. Everyone is happy. When even a small amount of acid from the cider is introduced, it will balance the condition in the stomach. This can be used before a meal for those who are lacking hydrochloric acid.

Apple Cider Vinegar is good for so many things from dissolving the calcium off the arteries to cleaning up skin problems, so I will leave this wonderful herb for later.

Besides Apple Cider Vinegar for the stomach, I like Ginger. Ginger tea is so soothing. For motion sickness or morning sickness, ginger tea comes to the rescue and soothes the area, with no chemical side effects to upset the system. Even pregnant women can use ginger with no harm to baby.

While on a boat trip with my husband, I found him working very hard to handle the motion of the boat. As soon as we docked, I ran to the resort kitchen and asked for a small piece of Ginger, put it into a glass of water and took it back to him. In a very short time he was back to normal.

At our house, we have found that five Fennel seeds chewed after a gassy meal are very helpful. Fennel will eliminate the gas. Fennel can also be made into a tea to help this condition. When one has a colic baby, a couple drops of fennel tea will allow everyone to get back to normal. Sometimes we combine Catnip tea with fennel for colic and everyone is happy.

Fennel is a very easy plant to grow and it is quite biblical in so far as when you plant one seed, 50 or more are returned to you on that one plant. According to Mrs. Grieves, "Pliny had much faith in its medicinal properties, according no less than twenty-two remedies to it." (Pliny being a Roman Scholar who wrote 37 volumes called *Historia Naturalis*. A.D. 62-79)

Some of the things that Fennel is said to be helpful with are: Nausea, Fleas, Inflamed eyes, Diarrhea in infants, Coughs, Congestion, Cancer – After Radiation and Chemotherapy, Hernias. It will increase breast milk

Phyllis Heitkamp Master Herbalist

for nursing moms, and it is good for Backaches, is said to help with PMS (More about this later). It is good for Toothaches and Spasms, just to name a few of the many things that Fennel can be used for.

Hanna mentioned that Grape leaves aid in the digestion process and they will prevent salmonella and botulism. Dandelion leaves are also helpful in aiding the digestion. She did mention that people who have trouble digesting wheat or gluten need Pantothenic Acid. The additional benefit of increasing this B vitamin (Pantothenic) is that it aids the Adrenals and that it lowers the body cholesterol. These last two facts are coming from Dr. Atkins' <u>Vita-Nutrient Solutions</u> book.

I have had people ask about what herbs would help a sore esophagus after they get the stomach working right and the acid no longer backs up on them. I have suggested Slippery Elm. There are lozenges that you can buy but they aren't as helpful as opening a capsule and just sucking on the herb allowing it to turn to liquid and slide down the throat. Slippery Elm is great at creating mucus that clings to the walls of an area and starts the healing. Slippery Elm is great in the stomach because it will cling there too instead of rushing on. The taste is somewhat like maple syrup.

We use Cayenne caps at our house for headaches because it balances out the blood pressure but it could be used to heal the stomach too. My husband called one day to say that his secretary had a headache and all he had was Cayenne. It seems that she has ulcers so he wanted to know if it would be OK for her to take this. I told him that it would not hurt her, in fact, it might even help. People who are serious about getting rid of them have used Cayenne for ulcers. I know it alkalizes the blood but it might also cauterize the area or kill the bacteria that are creating the ulcer. And yes, you will feel some discomfort but then when the doctor takes a biopsy of that area, you are going to feel more than "some discomfort" and in more areas than just the stomach.

Maybe here is a good place to talk about taking herbal capsules. I have had people tell me that they can't "do" herbs because they always taste them forever after they have swallowed the capsule. Most people do not know how to take a capsule. A capsule is taken with a swallow of water. This gets it into the stomach and then it sits there while the water that was taken with it, leaves. Now we have the contents of the capsule floating on the stomach acid. The proper way to take herbal capsules is to swallow the capsule with the mouthful of water and wait for a few minutes before

The Simplicity of Herbal Health

drinking the rest of the glass of water. What we are doing is making the tea (infusion) in the stomach. We are pulling the constituents of the herb out into the stomach instead of the teacup.

It is the same way with Cayenne. This capsule will open and needs to be mixed with water for the full benefit but most people don't do this and they get the burning sensation in the stomach area. When taken properly, Cayenne is a wonderful and useful herb.

It is very accepted in today's medicinal community that ulcers are caused by the Helicobacter pylori bacteria. It took the medical community a long time to recognize this bacteria. (At our house we call this the Helicopter bacteria.) There are many herbs that destroy bacteria - Black Walnut tincture or Goldenseal or Chaparral or Garlic are just a few. There are many more. Bacteria have been known to evolve to the point of being resistant to the chemicals used on them but plants have evolved too. The Goldenseal of 10 years ago might not handle the bacteria of today but today's Goldenseal would. What was used on the "helicopter" yesterday might not work tomorrow.

According to David Christopher, Director of the School of Natural Healing in Springville, Utah, only two things go directly into the blood stream through the stomach walls. They are aspirin and alcohol. Everything else must travel to the intestines and be absorbed through those walls. This is important to understand because we find that by making an alcoholic tincture, we can get an herbal preparation to "act fast" on the body by getting into the blood quickly.

* * *

Additional notes to this area: 2 teaspoonfuls of Apple Cider vinegar in 4 ounces of water will handle food poisoning, according to Hanna Kroeger, and aluminum can also cause stomach ulcers.

Another thing that is connected with the stomach area is Salmonella. When I went to study with Hanna Kroeger in Colorado, I signed in and got sick that night. My sister Betty, who had agreed to do this study with me, said that she would get Hanna. I didn't want to bother Hanna before she started her classes but my sister insisted.

Hanna came to our room and checked me out. She told me that I had salmonella and went to get something. She came back with a bottle of liquid and told me to put 15 drops of this in some water and take it. I did. I was supposed to do this again in another hour. She left, going back to the classroom where she was about to start teaching.

My sister left for class and I was there feeling wiped out. After about 15 minutes I was feeling better. I decided to take a shower and get dressed. Within 30 minutes, I felt fine and ready to go so I put the next 15 drops into some water and took off for class. I missed the introductions but I got all the rest of the information for that day.

My sister told me that she was grateful that I had volunteered to find out if this stuff really worked. We joked but we did find out something valuable. Vibrationals really do work. (See Introduction for information on vibrationals) Had I gone to the hospital, they would have pumped my stomach and kept me there for observation the whole morning.

We learned that Salmonella happens mainly in the stomach and Hanna's vibrational for that is great. She also has a vibrational called *60-33*. It handles Shigella and my sister likes to carry this one in her purse.

I have an Internet printout dated December of 2000, put out by the Associated Press and it states that, "E. coli Outbreak Now Confirmed In 3 States." It talks about recalling 1.1 millions pounds of ground beef prepared in Green Bay, Wisconsin that was contaminated with this. I am not going to comment on this state of affairs but will at this point mentions a common herb, Cinnamon has been known to handle this problem. Cinnamon is a bark on a trees and it will "take out" E. coli. I joke about the fact that everyone who eats out should eat the cinnamon buns, but here is a wonderful little herb that can handle this problem.

The Simplicity of Herbal Health

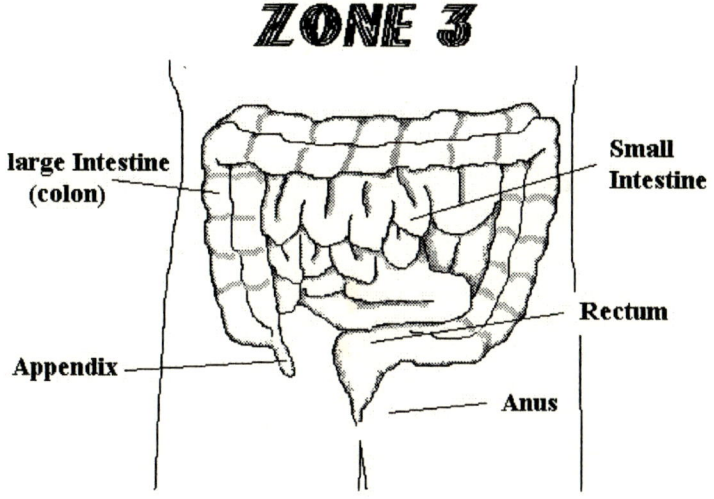

This brings us to Zone III

The first part of the intestine is called the duodenum and is about 10 inches long. It is in this area that the digestive juices from the liver and the pancreas enter the intestine. It is also the area where most of the activity of digesting food occurs.

It is this area that takes a real beating when it comes to antibiotics, as they tend to kill the entire flora community except for Candida Albicans. When this happens, Candida notices that there is more room to expand so it does and does and does. Soon the whole intestinal tract is loaded with Candida. It then expands even more by drilling holes in the intestinal walls and becomes a systemic problem that is misdiagnosed as everything from lupus to arthritis. The holes that Candida drills are small but do allow some small food particles to get through, which is not part of the design. Now we have food that starts decaying in the wrong place or tiny proteins that get into places where they were never meant to be, and we are having more problems. Homogenized milk consists of just such tiny proteins. Proteins are supposed to be absorbed as amino acids into the body, not floating around in the intestinal cavity as whole protein.

Phyllis Heitkamp Master Herbalist

After taking antibiotics, most people experience diarrhea because the system is so out of balance. The medical profession is starting to recognize this as a problem but for a while everything was treated with antibiotics.

A lady called me and told me that she wanted to know what to do for the diarrhea that she had since her return from Las Vegas a month earlier. She went to the Doctor and he gave her an antibiotic but it wasn't helping. I suggested Marshmallow and Slippery Elm capsules would be helpful and because herbs are taken 3 to 4 times a day, I recommended that she start immediately with one capsule of each 4 times that day. She said that she would do that after she finished her prescription of…you guessed it, antibiotics. I explained what was happening and said that I would start on the herbs now! In one day, just one day, she called to tell me that the diarrhea had stopped and should she continue to use the herbs. The answer is yes.

Marshmallow Root and Slippery Elm are called my "Big Guns" because they clean up old wounds. I have even used them to clean up gangrene. We will be discussing them more as we go along.

Fennel and Catnip will work for gas in the intestinal area as well as it did in the stomach.

Ginger is a good herb for healing the intestinal tract and brings the right nutrition to the area.

Goldenseal is also used as a healer for the intestinal tract. The nutrition in each herb gives the body building blocks.

According to Dr. Tyler, Goldenseal might be good for a few "canker sores and other conditions causing sore mouth." But he goes on to say in the two paragraphs that he has on Goldenseal that; "lacking any modern clinical studies dealing with the safety and efficacy of Goldenseal when used internally, it is necessary to agree with Sollmann that ingestion of the herb 'has few, if any rational indications.'" (This reference came from <u>A Manual of Pharmacology</u> by T. Sollmann written in 1948)

I looked in Dr. James Dukes book <u>The Green Pharmacy</u>, and just the index under Goldenseal, I find: "As Antiseptic, For treatment of Athlete's foot, bladder, infections, Canker sores, Chronic Fatigue syndrome, Colds and

The Simplicity of Herbal Health

flu, Earache, Fungal infections, Intestinal parasites, Pneumonia, Sinusitis, Sties, Tinnitus, Vaginitis, Viral infections, Wounds, Yeast infections."

It is my feeling that if Dr. Tyler was correct, Goldenseal would still be a prevalent herb and not as endangered as it is presently.

* * *

Parasites that make it through our defense system end up in the intestine and create many problems that get out of hand. There are three types of parasites; flat worms, round worms, and single cell parasites. We will be mentioning the two other types of parasites from time to time in this book, but the round worm category contains: Ascaris, Hookworm, Toxocara, Tapeworm, Whipworm, Dog Heartworm, Thread worms (Pin worms), and Trichinosis. (Information from <u>Parasites, The Enemy Within</u> by Kroeger.)

One of the flat parasites that act on this area is the Intestinal Fluke. Hanna mentions that these are hard to recognize but when we have rumbling noises and the feces are not solid, Intestinal flukes could be the problem. She has developed a vibrational remedy that handles this problem.

Parasites can be found in every area of the body, from the brain to the legs. Hanna Kroeger mentioned that most doctors are just starting to recognize this fact. She mentioned that medical texts written in the early 1900's talked about parasites but as we got more sophisticated through the years, we thought we were too "clean" to have parasites. She mentioned that even a small amount of vinegar in water every day would help to eliminate parasites.

Dr. Hulda Clark recognizes that parasites are the cause of most illnesses from HIV to skin problems according to her books. We are drawing in some of these problems because of the chemicals in our lives. Dioxin is used as a lawn spray, a pesticide and a herbicide. It ends up in the intestine. Hanna suggested using mustard seeds to remove dioxin. It can come into the body through bare feet, it goes directly to the kernel of the corn, and it attracts whipworm and virus. It has been known to cause birth defects and can go to the brain causing headaches. The next time you see a lawn that has little signs on it telling you that it has been sprayed for something, take the long way around or eat 10 to 15 mustard seeds. Hanna believed that the mustard seeds would keep you from getting AIDs. Chemicals are so integrated into our lives. She suggested that people with allergies, sinus problems and asthma be checked for Dioxin.

There are many herbs that will help eliminate these unwanted guests. One such herb is Wormwood. This herb is hard on the body so for the most part we take it in combination with other herbs. A nice Wormwood combination is good to use. On doing some research in Duke's Database, I noticed a property in Wormwood called "Vanillic Acid" and Dr. Duke says that it is "Ascaricide." So here is a property in Wormwood that targets one of the round worms specifically.

Dr. Duke's Database told me that Asparagus shoots have three properties in them that are "parasiticide". He says that Tarragon has two properties that do this, Coffee has two properties, Black Pepper has two, Okra has one, Yarrow has one, Onion has one, Cashews have one, Pineapple has one, Dill has one, Celery root has one and horseradish has one property that is "parasiticide."

In treating parasites, it is wise to remember that they are cyclical and active only around the full moon therefore when treating them we start five days before a full moon and continue 10 days afterwards. Then we stop for the next 15 days, while they are dormant and start taking our treatment 5 days before the next full moon. The first time we killed the adults and the second time we killed the larva.

My favorite herb is Black Walnut Tincture. I told you earlier that this was antiseptic but now I am saying that it is also antiparasitic along with being antifungal and because I know that it will get rid of warts, which are virus, it is antiviral. As an after thought, it might not be such a good thing to live on Black Walnut Tincture because as I mentioned, it also kills fungus and it will rid the body of some of the good flora but it is a great healer.

Previously I mentioned that some parasites do not stay in the intestinal tract and we will be bumping into them as we go along but the ones that do stay are very content to eat our food and put their waste in our intestines. They also multiply and the more we feed them, the happier they are. Herbal combinations will get rid of them.

One gentleman had a tapeworm and it took three months to get it out. Why that long? Because as we have mention, parasites are active around the full moon. This means if a stool sample is taken at the new moon, nothing will be found.

* * *

What do we need to do to keep the colon healthy? We need to drink lots of water. We already discussed why water is important but in the colon water is absorbed into the system. And here is where we find food plastered to the walls of the colon. The body demands the water/liquid from food, if that is all it is getting. We have milk/latex painted on the walls of the colon as the body used the water in the milk, which was the only liquid this person drank. WATER, WATER, we need WATER. Juices will help supply us with water. But coffee and sodas are diuretics. They take more water out than they put in.

Remember when we were in second grade and the teacher mixed up some flour, salt and water and the class made a map of the United States? We put the Rocky Mountains where they belonged and the Mississippi River down the middle. Don't forget the Great Lakes and how about Salt Lake? Then the teacher said that tomorrow we could paint this map. By the next day it was dry and we painted the East Coast green with rivers of blue. It looked so nice and we were so proud of our relief map with mountains and rivers.

Well, that is just what we have in our Colon. We eat "dead" grains in the form of bread and pasta and if we aren't drinking enough water to wash them through, they form the mountains and rivers that clog up the colon. And if a mountain has been sitting there long enough, it might depress that area into diverticulitis, or pockets of decaying matter.

How about the truck driver who has "dun-laps" disease? His stomach "dun-laps" over his belt. This is the transverse colon that has about 5 or more years of mountains made of decaying food. Why does this man eat so much at every sitting? He is starving. The food that he does eat goes in one end and out the other. There is no connection with the intestinal lining where osmosis can take place. The man is hungry!

I tell my students that we consume three "trucks-full" of food every day, why would it be healthy to have only one "truck-load" leaving a day. We need to have two or more bowel movements a day to be healthy. A healthy newborn baby will have to have a diaper change every time it eats.

Phyllis Heitkamp Master Herbalist

* * *

Unlike a car, we are self-healing. We can rebuild if 10% of an organ is left after surgery or if 10% of it is healthy. But we need to assist the body with this. What do we need? We need "clean" Fruits, Vegetables, Whole Grains, Nuts and Seeds. I am not saying that anyone should become a vegetarian to be healthy but these 5 things provide the nutrition to get and stay healthy.

Dr. John R. Christopher says that there is only one dis-ease in the body and that is constipation/congestion. What is constipated/congested? Is it the Bowels? That is where we usually think of constipation but it could be the veins or the arteries or the nerves or even at the cellular level. The medical profession has a name for every dis-ease, but all one needs to figure out is why isn't that area getting nutrition or getting the toxins out? If the cells in an area are getting food and able to dispose of its waste, they will stay healthy and rebuild.

The Simplicity of Herbal Health

Where To Start

Atomists (Doctors) feel that they can control the body from the outside with chemicals or whatever they think the body needs.

Vitalists (herbalists) believe the body has a mind of its own. It is aware that there is a problem in this area or that area and that more calcium or whatever is needed in that area.

Have you ever wondered why some people catch everything and other people walk into situations where there is illness but never get sick?

Germs are everywhere. They are on the book you are reading. They are on your skin. They are in the air. They have the job of feeding on garbage. They are like flies in so far as they clean up the junk that isn't supposed to be there. They are like bugs on a plant. You won't find bugs on a healthy plant, only on ones that need to be cleaned up or recycled. Well, germs have a purpose too and that is to clean up the excessive "junk" that is in our bodies. When we are eating healthy foods, the macrophages are able to handle the excessive toxins that come in, but when we overload the body with mucus (Ice Cream or Dairy) the job becomes overwhelming for the macrophages and we end up getting sick. Is the body working when we are sick? Yes, very much so. It has made the environment conducive to germs to help get rid of the bacterial overload in that area.

To turn a five day flu into a one day flu, (and it can be done) one must help the body incubate the germs so the toxins are cleaned up faster. Why incubate germs? If we have more garbage collectors to clean up the place, it will be cleaned up faster. How do we incubate germs? The body knows. It builds a fever. I know, you have been taught to kill the fever fast with some chemical. But the natural way the body handles this is to build a fever. Now we have been taught from early childhood that fevers are dangerous. What we had been taught was right in so far as a **high dry fever is deadly**, as it can cause brain damage but a **high WET fever is safe**.

When I started to learn about herbal health, I told my daughter that this was so foreign to my way of thinking. She just reminded me that I only had to agree until I got the degree. As I learned more and more, it started to make sense to me. Now I understand how it works and not only agree but try to help others understand how this works.

How do we build a safe fever? We start with a steamy room and a hot bath. We even put herbs in the bath water if we wish. Peppermint is a great one for the hot bath, as it tends to release the aromatic oils for the person to breathe in along with the steam. Then we supply the body with lots of hot liquids. Some of the teas suggested are Yarrow, Ginger, Cayenne, and even Peppermint tea. All of these herbs stimulate the body's systems. Make sure that a couple of pints of the tea of choice are drunk. When the person tells you that they have had enough, Dr. Christopher would ask them to tip their head, if the tea runs out of their ears, they have had enough. This is a **high wet** fever. Wet inside and out. He suggests that they stay in the hot water for "as long as possible" or at least one half hour then get tucked into bed to sweat it out.

I have used peppermint with children but Yarrow is such a wonderful herb for the start of any problem. I have found that when my husband tells me that he has a tickle in his throat and he thinks he is getting "something", a cup of yarrow tea will handle it on the spot. The next day when I ask how he feels, he wonders why I am asking -- the tickle being only a memory.

* * *

We need to clean out the body and the way to do that is by starting with the bowels. If the bowels are congested, no matter what we try to heal will release its toxins but because they can't get out of the body, they will recycle as something else.

There was a gentleman who had poison ivy blisters up to his knee on one leg. He was in a lot of discomfort. I suggested that he make a tea of Stinging Nettle and apply the tea to the leg with a cloth. I also asked him to call me if he had a problem. He called about five hours later to tell me that the Nettle worked really well. He said that the bubbles went down right away along with the itching and that the redness went away after a few hours but he broke out with a rash on his back. The toxins could not get out. What was constipated? Was it his bowels? Kidneys? Liver? I don't know, all I know is that his body needed to be cleaned out.

We start by cleaning out the intestines and colon. Every herbalist, every health food store has formulas for the intestine. My students want

The Simplicity of Herbal Health

to know how they will know if their colon is cleaned out. I tell them that if they are having two or more bowel movements a day, they can move on to cleaning up other areas of the body. I found that while I was working on my bowels, I got diarrhea. This is very common because we are cutting the stored, dried food away from the walls of the colon. This sometimes causes cramping as it pulls away and exposes the cells of this area to food matter. Some of these cells haven't been exposed for years. This dried food matter sometimes causes a dam in the colon and diarrhea happens. This is not the time to stop. We continue using the herbal combination and drinking lots of water. By drinking lots of water, we are softening the matter and it will be released. When most people get diarrhea they stop the process, thus creating a worse situation.

We will talk about the other areas of the body in other chapters. In this chapter we want to find out about herbs that work on the intestines. The following is a list of a few and how they work.

* * *

Cathartic herbs according to Dr. John Christopher in his <u>School of Natural Healing</u> book, are herbs that "hasten intestinal evacuation. Some cause activity of the peristalsis and some stimulate glandular secretion of the intestine. Some of these agents have an affinity for a particular area. Botanical cathartics not only speed up the physical evacuation processes but they are also powerful healers in cleansing, strengthening and toning the malfunctioning tissue and organs."

My favorite is Cascara sagrada because it doesn't act like other laxatives but activates the peristalsis muscles that are around the intestine to create a snake like action to move waste matter along. It is a gentle cathartic.

Another good one is Licorice. Licorice acts on the liver and helps to release bile to activate the intestinal action. It is not only mild but tastes great. One of my students told me that her grandchild was having one bowel movement a week. I suggested this herb. I have only found it without sugar in Panda so I suggested that they give this child one piece of Panda, 3 to 4 times a day as her medicine. (Panda is also high in Molasses)

At the next class this grandmother told me that it was working and the child was have a bowel movement once a day.

Activating the liver is a very good thing so Barberry is another herb that is so helpful in this area. According to Dr. Christopher, it is "unequal as a corrector of liver secretions and it expels and removes morbid waste matter from the stomach and bowels." We will be talking about this herb more in future chapters.

Another that can be suggested is Butternut bark or White Walnut. This is a very beneficial tonic for the entire intestinal tract and is recommended for the "aged, middle-aged and weakly children where no drastic action is tolerated," according to Dr. Christopher.

Others are Mountain Flax, Turkey Rhubarb, Mandrake or May Apple, Wahoo, but these tend to be hard on the body and need to be taken with caution and in combination with other herbs or in small dosages.

* * *

We want things to work fast. Herbs work fast on people with clean bodies. This doesn't mean that we shower every day, it means that we clean up inside the body so the toxins can get out and the nutrition can get in.

When one takes a drug, this blocks the process. Drugs give the body false messages. Aspirin tells the body that there is no fever or pain. The body knows that the knee hurts and it sends a bigger message to the T-cells, then we take more drugs to turn the pain off. What we need to do is handle the problem. In my class I tell my students that we need to answer the door before turning off the doorbell. The doorbell is just telling us that there is a problem to be dealt with. When we take a painkiller, we are trying to tell the body that it is wrong, that there isn't any problem and down the road the problem gets bigger.

The first place to start herbal health is by cleaning out the bowels. We need to correct our diets to include the five things that we have mentioned, Fruits, Vegetables, Whole grains, Nut and Seed, along with herbs, and distilled water. We need to exercise everyday even if it is just going up and down the stairs a few extra times a day. Most of all we need to "heal" our thinking. We need to be more positive. Do more fun things. Be around people who are happy, positive people that are doing fun things.

Life is good and our bodies can be healed of all dis-ease. The design is there.

Chapter 1 - Resources

Atkins, Robert C., MD, *Dr. Atkins' Vita-Nutrient Solution,* A Fireside Book, 1998, 407 pg.

Batmangheilidj, F., MD, *Your Body's Many Cries for Water,* Global Health Solutions, Inc., Falls Church, VA, 1992, 182 pg.

Blake, Steven, Globalherb V2.0, California, 2003

Christopher, John R., Dr., *School Of Natural Healing,* Christopher Publication, Springville, UT. , 1976, 724 pg., 1-800-372-8255

Christopher, John R., ND, MH., *Regenerative Diet,* Christopher Publications, Springville,UT. 1982, 275 pg., www.snh.cc

Duke, James A, Ph.D., Dr. Duke's Phytochemical and Ethnobotanical Database, 2002

Duke, James A., Ph.D., *The Green Pharmacy,* Rodale Press, Emmaus, PA, 1997, 508 pg.

Grieves, Maude, Mrs. *A Modern Herbal,* Dover Publications, Inc., NY.,1971, 902 pg.

Kelly, Penny, *The Elves of Lily Hill Farms: A Partnership with Nature,* Authors Choice Press, Lincoln, NE. 1997, 240 pg

Kroeger, Hanna, Rev. *Basic Causes of Modern diseases and How To Remedy Them,* Hay House, Carlsbad, CA. 1984, 162 pg

Kroeger, Hanna Rev., *Parasites, the Enemy Within,* Hanna Kroeger Publications, 1991, 62 pg.

Tyler, Varro E., Ph.D., *Herbs of Choice,* Pharmaceutical Productions Press, Binghamton, NY, 1994, 209 pg.

Chapter II
Tea time

Before starting this chapter, please purchase a small ginger root from the local grocery store. Good, now we are ready to start. It is time to create another **infusion** (tea). This time we are going to start by slicing the ginger root into thin quarter-sized pieces and putting 5 of them into a cup. Then we pour hot water over this ginger root and let it set (steep) for a few minutes before drinking it.

Ginger is such a great herb. It can be used to control nausea and because it is so mild, it can be used by pregnant women for morning sickness. It's a tea that can be used for motion sickness. One can purchase candied ginger and chew on it for this purpose while traveling. It is good for upset stomachs, stomachaches and even the pain of a stomach ulcer. I even read where it can be used as an antidote for mushroom poisoning but I have not put it to this test. What I have tested it on is its ability to handle gas in the body. It does work well for this.

Ginger is also a stimulant. This means that it will heat the body by getting the blood moving faster. Therefore it is good for circulation, heart disease, fatigue, depression, and learning problems. It has been used for cancers because it gets the blood moving in stagnated areas. I have used it for my chronic sinus congestion with much success. It help with constipation.

It will act as a lead herb. As a lead herb it is put into herbal combinations to help move the herbal remedies to where they are most needed in the body. This is good because another talent of Ginger is to stop pain. So by getting a healing combination to painful areas, as in arthritis, one can enjoy life again.

Externally, Ginger can be put in the bathtub and it will control the discomfort of hives. I like to take an old clean sock and make it into a large tea bag. I cut the Ginger up and put it into the sock, tie or put a rubber band on the top and let the sock float in the tub before I climb in. This is so soothing.

Phyllis Heitkamp Master Herbalist

How can Ginger do so much? This is because herbs don't have a specific job to do. They give the body what it needs to heal. It is the body that does the healing. I checked with my computer program, Globalherb, and found about 30 things that are available in Ginger, some of which are; Chromium - .0006% (these are called trace minerals because the body only needs a trace of them), Manganese, Magnesium, Niacin, Lecithin, Nickel, Selenium, Sulfur, Copper, Zinc and more. As you can see, Ginger has a lot to offer and you just had a cup of Ginger tea.

The Liver

This chapter is mostly about the liver, which is one of the most important and hardest working organs in the body. (And everyone thinks that it is the heart muscle that works the hardest.) Let's find out what the liver does.

Did you know that it breaks down all the chemicals that are in your body, turning them into bile and releasing them out of the body? This means that every time you take an aspirin, the chemicals in the aspirin have to go all the way through your body and find their way to the liver, where they are broken down and added to the bile made by the liver, then sent out of the body.

Now, that sounds simple. But aspirin isn't the only chemical that we introduce to the liver.

It has to break down hormones made by the body, both male and female hormones, on a daily basis. PMS isn't a natural thing. It means that the liver is so busy breaking down the chemicals from our food, or in our air and in the ground that we walk on that the liver has to put hormonal chemicals somewhere in the body while it works very hard to keep us alive. Then the next month comes and now more hormones are there...we have overload. PMS speaks of a constipated liver. The hormones are being recycled instead of gotten rid of. Excessive amounts of estrogen have been linked with breast cancers, blood clots, strokes and uterine cancers. Did you know that the liver could still create hormones for the body even after a hysterectomy? A lot of organs have the ability to use the phytosterols in plants and make hormones out of them. We will be touching on that later in this book. There are other symptoms of liver-hormonal overload. Male pattern baldness is related to excessive hormones as is prostate swellings.

In addition to that, the liver has to break down the chemicals created when we "feel". When we are "In Love", we are "In Love" all the way to the ends of our fingers because we create chemicals that give us this feeling. When we are angry with the driver in front of us, we feel anger all the way to our toes because we have created that chemical. We go from happy to angry to sad to depressed and all of those "feeling chemicals" have to be broken down and gotten rid of.

So what does the medical profession do for chemical overload? They give us more chemicals, Prozac or Paxel or some other chemical. What can a liver do?

Dr. John Christopher called the Liver the cesspool of the body and said that no one should ever eat it. This is where all the poisons go to be detoxed. When an animal gets hurt, the puss and debris go to the liver to be neutralized and sent out of the body. The liver will pull the poisons from all the glands and organs like a magnet and put them into bile. This bile will act as a laxative on the intestine.

When the liver is in trouble, the body is in trouble. Did you know that "age spots" or "liver spots" are also a sign that the liver is in trouble, as is jaundice. Hanna has said that when the body turns yellow, a virus has been active in the body for the last 5 years. We need to help the liver. When it is in trouble, Dr. Christopher suggested working from both the inside and the outside. On the outside he suggests a very warm **fomentation** of Castor Oil (Described below) applied over the liver area for 30 minutes and then alternate with cold tap water for 5 minutes. Never take Castor Oil internally (according to Dr. Christopher), as it is poisonous to the body that way.

I had to use this fomentation on a friend of mine who was very depressed. The Doctors had given her medication for the depression but it wasn't helping and she just seemed to get worse. When tested, she was found to be loaded with mercury. She decided to chelate the mercury out of her body and in doing so, her liver became overloaded. This is very painful and my friend had to stop the chelation process until she could get her liver healthy again.

Her mother asked me how she got the mercury? I tried to think of ways that we get it, perhaps in dental work or printed matter. Then a month later, in the local newspaper, there was an article stating that the air in the surrounding area was 10% higher in mercury than the EPA allows but also stated that it was not a problem unless one was eating the local fish. Isn't that interesting? Mercury is a vapor in the air, why would we not be breathing it? Not a problem unless we are eating the local fish? I doubt that.

Hanna mentioned that Mercury is in the core of many vaccines (Herbalists do not believe in vaccines as this means puncturing our hermetic seal and putting foreign material where it doesn't belong.) Mercury is also found in fly sprays, most medicine, scar tissue and a lot of times in our tailbone, according to Hanna. She created a couple of vibrationals to help with this problem.

* * *

Fomentation

What is a **fomentation**? A fomentation is made by putting an infusion (tea), oil or some other preparation into a bowl, placing a cotton or flannel cloth in the solution and soaking up as much as the material will hold. Wring out enough to keep it from dripping and apply it to the afflicted area.

To force the body to accept the herbal solution or preparation, we add heat. This can be anything from a hot water bottle to "hot rocks." The latter is from a story that Dr. Christopher told about information he found in some old books. I sometimes heat a bath towel in the oven and place it over the area being treated.

So what is the difference between a fomentation and a **poultice**? As you see in this description, the only thing being used on the body is the liquid in a fomentation. In a poultice, one would apply the soaked herb directly to the skin or by way of putting the soaked herb between two pieces of material and then applying it to the skin.

* * *

Dr. Christopher suggested that the liver could rebuild if it is cleansed and nourished. On the inside of the body, he suggests using 3 parts of Barberry root along with 1 part of Fennel or Wild Yam. This is made into an infusion so one would drink one-half cup every hour.

Barberry is a wonderful herb. The best part of it is the fact that it is bitter. Bitter is the property that activates the liver. Dr. James A. Duke talked about Barberry's antioxidant properties. He mentions that antioxidants neutralize free radicals that damage cells. Dr. Adkins explained that cells need oxygen to live but having too much of a good thing is bad too. When there is an excess of oxygen in the body, cells break down faster than is normal and the area is at risk for many things from heart problems, cancers, arthritis, Alzheimer's disease, and even premature aging.

Barberry has so many uses and they aren't all connected with the liver. It is good for the blood, the spleen, and the intestines, even helping the gums. It works as a diuretic on the kidneys. Because it is so good with the liver and the liver is so important, it is said to help with fevers, infections, boils, high blood pressure, typhoid and jaundice.

"Barberry contains an alkaloid called Berberin which dilates blood vessels," according to Jack Ritchason. He also mentions that this same substance is found in Goldenseal and that they are both strong antiseptics. Berberin is said to support the health of the mucous membranes and because of this, it might be used as a gargle for a sore throat. This would take some doing because the bitter property of this herb is potent. I think I would have to acquire the ability to do this. There are other milder herbs that I might use for this purpose.

What are some of the herbs that can be used to help the liver rebuild or heal? Dr. James Duke talked about the fact that "bitter is better" in regard to the liver.

Dr. Christopher has a wonderful formula that cleans up the liver and gallbladder so that the body is working the way it was designed to work. He puts together; 3 parts - Berberis vulgaris (Barberry), 1 part – Wild Yam, 1 part – Cramp Bark, 1 part – Fennel seed, 1 part – Ginger, 1 part – Catnip, 1 part – Peppermint. He calls it his *Liver & Gall Bladder Formula*.

Barberry isn't the only herb that is helpful at supporting the liver, my favorite is Milk Thistle, but there is also Grape seed extract and Mountain Grape, a cousin to Barberry. Other powerful herbs for the liver are Cascara Sagrada, Club Moss, Gentian and Black Cohosh. Garlic is a good liver tonic.

* * *

Milk Thistle has been used for everything from hepatitis to cancer, with diabetes and mushroom poisoning in between. Milk Thistle is rich in bioflavonoids. (When Vitamins were first discovered, Bioflavonoids were called Vitamin P.) There are antioxidants and free radical scavengers available in this wonderful herb. Well, in fact, Dr. Dukes Database shows almost 60 constituents in Milk Thistle, from Calcium to Zinc and everything in between. He shows some of the properties of these constituents, like Apigenin being antiviral or Magnesium having anti-stroke properties. This last bit of information was referenced from <u>Syndrome X – The Complete Nutritional Program To Prevent And Reverse Insulin Resistance</u>. (See bibliography for Challem, J, ect.)

Cholesterol isn't the only thing that can cause high blood pressure. There are high triglycerides, and hardening of the arteries (Calcium deposits on the walls of the arteries). So we need to find what is creating the problem and handle that situation.

When my husband came home with a prescription for high triglycerides, (Here is another case of adding drugs to the body to give the liver more work.) I asked him if that was what he was going to take? He responded with, "Well, do you have something better?" I suggested a bottle of Milk Thistle. (Herbs are food, Milk Thistle is a plant like celery or carrots.) He told me that he would take the Milk Thistle capsules for one month and then have another test and if the test showed that his triglycerides were still high, he was taking the prescription. I agreed. One month later the Walgreen's bag with the staples still on, was dumped into the trash. Ten dollars worth of Milk Thistle and no further damage to the liver, the tests were back in range.

With the triglycerides, one could cut back on simple carbohydrates. In a later chapter, we will be talking about simple carbohydrates as opposed to complex carbohydrates. I find that most of us don't know the difference.

Dr. Atkins calls sugar the "antinutrient." He says that "It is 100 percent carbohydrate and therefore contains no vitamins or minerals." We will be talking about sugars later in this book but Triglycerides, though needed to supply the lipid fats to the cells, should not be made from raw sugar but rather from the glucose in our foods.

* * *

There is a story that Doctor Christopher used to tell about a little girl that had a very bad leg infection.

The parents were herbalists so they used a lot of herbs but the problem got worse. They finally took the child to the doctor and the doctor said that it was gangrene, maybe even bone cancer. He thought that he would have to amputate. The parents were very upset and asked if there wasn't something else that they could try first. The doctor finally agreed to put the child on antibiotics.

As herbalists, the parents knew that antibiotics throw the body out of balance and create even worse problems, so they didn't give them to the child. The doctor called to check on the child and asked if the antibiotics had helped. The parents told him that they weren't doing the antibiotics.

The doctor called the Health Department and Social Services as the parents were, in his estimation, neglecting the child's welfare.

The mother took the child and ran away. She called Dr. Christopher from where they stayed the first night and he suggested Garlic, Goldenseal and his wonderful *Compete Tissue Formula*. (We will hear more about this formula.)

But the child didn't get better so when the mother called to tell him this, he suggested that she feed the child only carrot juice for a week. As much as the child wanted but nothing else. The second week, she was to feed only grape juice to the child. And the third week, only apple juice. The mother went to a health food store, got a juicer and started making the juices. The fourth week, She was supposed to start over with the carrot juice but Mother and child came home and all was healing nicely. The juices provided the cleansing that the liver needed to handle the infection coming in its direction.

* * *

I once researched carrot on my herbal computer program and found that it contained four pages with thirty different nutrients on each page. Here is a master food. It cleanses and provides the body with building blocks on every front.

From Queen-Ann's lace to garden carrot, here is the king of foods.

Jethro Kloss said it best. "If carrots were used more extensively as a vegetable, they would prove of great benefit to mankind. Patients are often put on a carrot diet for a short period of time for cancer, liver, kidney and bladder troubles. Carrots are very useful in dropsy (Water retention), gravel in the bladder, painful urination, to increase the menstrual flow, and

The Simplicity of Herbal Health

in expelling worms from the bowels." He suggested carrot poultices for all kinds of skin problems.

Hanna had a lot of uses for carrots from blood builders and purifiers to weight loss. She suggested that using a poultice of grated carrots could be used for breast sores and even cold sores to mouth ulcers. The juice was used for a lot of things too. We know that it is good for the eyes, due to its high vitamin content but it is also good for the blood and lymph according to Hanna. She also suggested making a tea of carrot seeds and that drinking it as it "will remove tension from smooth muscles such as the intestines."

How did Carrot get into this book on herbs? Very simply because herbs are foods and foods are healing.

My neighbor had a lot of weeds in his yard and asked me what they were. I told him that I am an herbalist, not a botanist but I would identify some of them. I pulled up a Queen Ann's Lace and scraped the root. Then I asked him to smell it. He identified the family right away as carrot. Wild or tame, carrots are wonderful herbs.

* * *

Another herb that I like my students to taste is Licorice. Most of us remember that black candy we tasted as a child and we either liked it or we didn't. What we didn't know was that Licorice doesn't taste that way. The candy tasted of Anise or Fennel but not Licorice. My students are surprised to find that it doesn't taste like they remember it at all.

Licorice has been used for a long time for so many things. The medical profession says that these herbs haven't had clinical studies done on them to show what they can heal and what they can't. I guess that thousands of years of use just isn't good enough?

Did you know that Licorice roots were found in King Tutankhamen's tomb? Did you know that the armies of Alexander the Great carried Licorice roots with them? It allowed them to travel great distances on very little water because Licorice will allay thirst.

David and Fawn Christopher have done some research on Licorice and have come up with a lot of facts that I would like to mention. "Licorice is well known for its great healing powers for sore throats, coughs and bronchitis, but most people don't know that it is equally as good for irritation of the bowels and kidneys. It has been used for inflammation of the stomach, indigestion and even peptic ulcers. A Danish study shows that is it helpful for duodenal and peptic ulcers. In Colitis, the combination is 60% Slippery Elm and 40 % Licorice is great. Addison's disease, TB and even almost atrophied adrenal glands will respond to Licorice root. Cold Licorice tea is a coolant for the body". For this reason, according to David & Fawn Christopher, it is used in the iron industry. They also mention that it can be used for nighttime alertness without caffeine for those long drives late at night or for a night shift.

What is it about Licorice that is so great? Some research says that it is the glycyrrhetic acid and the saponins found in Licorice that works the wonders. The glycyrrhetic acid gives the body cortisone-like effects. For this reason Licorice has been used as a wash for skin problems. This acid is 50 time sweeter than sugar.

I recently received an e-mail link to <u>Nature News Service/ Macmillian Magazines Ltd 2003</u>. One of my students thought the information was something that I might be interested in. The article was titled, "Liquorice May Tackle SARS" It was written by Helen R. Pilcher and her article said that "High doses of liquorice extract, called glycyrrhizin, practically wiped out the SARS virus in infected monkey cells, finds virologist Jindrich Cinati of Frankfurt University Medical School, Germany. The drug is more potent than ribavirin, the most commonly used treatment for SARS." She goes on to explain how it works but mentioned that large amounts are needed. In this same article she talks about the fact that this compound, Glycyrrhizin "helps restore liver function in patients with Hepatitis C. It is currently being assessed as a treatment for HIV infection, as it slows the replication of the virus in cultured cells."

The saponins of licorice create suds that have soothing effect on the cells. It will soothe the whole GI tract along with the kidneys. It also helps loosen phlegm in the respiratory tract so the body can expel it.

I read where the Chinese use it for fevers and pain. They also use it mixed with honey for burns, boils and sores.

Dr. Duke talks about Licorice being used for Arthritis. He said that it has anti-inflammatory effects and is soothing to the system. He suggested a formula that would be very helpful -- 3 part Willow bark, (for the pain as willow has salicylic acid.) 2 parts Licorice for its anti-inflammatory effect and 1 part garlic. The garlic is to reduce the blood pressure that can increase when licorice is taken over a long period of time or in large amounts.

There have even been studies showing that one can chew on a Licorice root to help stop smoking.

Licorice seems to have so many uses from coughs to bronchitis to low estrogen. I have even read where it is good for people who do a lot of traveling, as it will help prevent jet lag.

Because of all these great things, Dr. John Christopher put Licorice into a lot of his formulas. He has it in his *Hormonal Changeese Formula,* because it also contains precursors to hormones. He has it in his *Blood Stream Formula* because it has been used for centuries in Europe as a blood purifier and he has it in his *Pancreas Formula,* because even though it is sweet, it contains no sugar.

Licorice is also a very mild laxative as mentioned in the last chapter.

I found Licorice tea to be helpful for menopausal symptoms. We will be discussing female health in a later chapter.

Adding Licorice tea to other teas that either have no flavor of their own or taste like grass, is a good way to get the nutrition we need but bypass the bitter or bad taste.

* * *

One of the hardest things for the liver to do is deal with all the chemicals in our world today. We were not designed to handle chemicals but all of the organs try to do this. Hanna has an herbal combination called *Chem-X*, which contains Black Tea, Condurango Bark, Red Clover, Yellow dock, Paprika, Chaparral, and Spikenard. It is designed to help the body with chemical constrictions or blockages.

Hanna also has two vibrationals called *Hepalpha and Hepbeta* that handle Hepatitis A & B, two infections that invade the liver.

Phyllis Heitkamp Master Herbalist

I also read where pectin can pull metals and chemicals out of the body. Perhaps that is why my husband gravitated to eating apples when he was detoxing from a past cigarette habit?

Hanna also suggested that cooked red potatoes, mashed and applying to the area of the liver as a poultice would help if the liver is swollen. She suggested cloves in regard to the liver, as being "Beneficial when swollen, hard, damaged or containing tumors."

She also says, " Apricots, and pineapple juice; used to detoxify liver and pancreas. Soak 1 pound of dried apricots in pineapple juice. Next morning, blend mixture and take this 2 days in a row."

Dr. Christopher suggests Black Radish, Dandelion, Goldenseal or Red Clover for Hepatitis.

One job of the liver is to store glucose and send it out, as the body needs it. Glucose is the fuel that our body runs on. This will be discussed more later in this book. The liver is important enough for everyone to assist it in helping us stay healthy.

The Simplicity of Herbal Health

The Lymph System

How do toxins get to the liver? They come in through the lymph system. And we don't do a very good job of keeping that system ready to handle the amount of "junk" that we need to release every day.

Dr. Christopher talked about the promise in the Bible that if the lymph and the liver are clean, they will save your life. He said that you can be bitten by a poisonous snake or take a poisonous chemical and it will go directly to the liver through the lymph system and pass out of the body in the bile. But what usually happens is that the poison gets as far as a lymph node and stops there because it has done such a good house cleaning, bringing all the "junk" that is in the lymph system down to the nodes and that creates a blockage. Then the poison will leave that area and get into the blood system and head for the heart. That is the end. These two systems are very different and if clean, they each do their jobs.

How do we clean up the lymph system? Dr. Christopher created a formula just for that. It consists of 3 parts Mullein and 1 part Lobelia. He talked about this formula as being good for healing glands, lymph glands being one of the many glands in our body.

I heard about this formula: 3 parts Mullein and 1 part Lobelia and thought, "My thyroid isn't working right. I wonder if this would heal it?" While taking classes with Hanna Kroeger, she said that if an organ is dead it would decay and poison the body so it would need to be taken out of the body, if it isn't dead, heal it. She just didn't tell me how to heal it. I had been taking Synthroid for 10 years. My thyroid wasn't dead, it just wasn't working right, so I decided to try this.

I started taking one Mullein/Lobelia capsule and one Synthroid a day. I continued this for 40 days. (Why 40? I really don't know but this felt like a good period of time.) At the end of the forty days, I put the Synthroid in my dresser drawer just in case I needed it later (always have a plan B). I continued to take the one Mullein/Lobelia capsule a day. After doing this for a few months, I started taking the Mullein/Lobelia a couple of times a week and then every other week until I now take it "as needed" or a couple of times a year.

Phyllis Heitkamp Master Herbalist

Yes, I did have a set back. About 2 months into this program, I woke up one morning with an enlarged thyroid but to my surprise, instead of running to those hidden Synthroid, I just doubled up on my *Glandular System Formula* (Mullein and Lobelia) and in a very short time, I was fine again.

Hanna suggested Lettuce and basil for swollen lymph glands. She suggested Echinacea for diseased lymph glands and to boost the lymph system, and she recommended cucumbers and bananas to increase the potassium in this area.

Mullein and Lobelia aren't the only things that one has to do for a thyroid problem. The first thing that Hanna would say is, " Get rid of fluoride." She mentioned that it weakens this organ. I have seen research in her book by Ernest Hodgson and Frank Guthrie that says, "Pronounced hyperglycemia and glucosuria are induced in rabbits by sodium fluoride. The Hyperglycemia is reversible by insulin." She also has a picture of Dr. John Yiamonsiamis's research on chromosome damage done by fluoride. Because of all of this information, she always said, "No Fluoride treatments!" She feels that it lowers the immune system by 95% in 12 hours. Let's see, that would mean that if I brush my teeth with fluoride toothpaste twice a day, I am running on about 10% of my ability to ward off infections. This would be reason enough for the medical system not to object having it in our water.

We have been tricked into thinking that fluoride is good for our health. A lot of cities have "drugged" their water without the consent of the people. We are rused into thinking it is good for our teeth. I have been told that more tooth decay is caused by Strep infection than anything else. Our bodies require Calcium Fluoride to stay healthy and what is in all the dental products? Sodium Fluoride! Did you know that there have even been children who have died in the dentist chair after a fluoride treatment? Insurance claims have been settled quietly. Sodium fluoride kills! From what I have read, it is worse than lead poisoning. It is also damaging to the thyroid as well as the parathyroid and thymus glands. Finding toothpaste without sodium fluoride is not easy but it can be done. A Dentist that attended my classes talked about the fact that you don't really need toothpaste to have healthy teeth, you just need to brush.

Hanna wrote about how sodium fluoride causes the Thymus gland to malfunction. As we get older, she says, problems will surface from this fact. One of the problems could be a cataract and another could be hearing

The Simplicity of Herbal Health

problems. She says that this is due to a rigidity that happens when the thymus shrinks.

The next thing that one needs to know about having a healthy thyroid is that it needs organic iodine to stay healthy. Did you notice that I said organic? The body will use inorganic material but we are created from organic material and therefore uses organic matter much easier. Sure we can get around with a plastic hip but if we rebuilt the bones, the body would like it much better (and this can be done too…Check in later chapters.)

Organic iodine can be found in Kelp. I find that just any kelp will work but as a better source, I like Dulse (a type of kelp). So what do we do when we live a long way from an ocean? Black Walnut hulls are a great source of organic iodine. It is the iodine that turns the hulls black as they oxidize.

Now that my thyroid is healed and no longer gives me trouble, I don't take anything on a regular basis but from time to time (maybe once a month) I treat this body with a day regiment of Mullein and Lobelia. I do the Black Walnut tincture more often because of all its other properties. We will be talking about Black Walnut later.

Phyllis Heitkamp Master Herbalist

Making a Decoction

It is time to talk about another herbal preparation and this one is called a **Decoction**. Decoctions are stronger than infusions and are usually made from harder plant parts such as roots or bark or even seeds.

The general proportions are 1 part herb to 16 parts water. When herbalists talk about parts, these can be cups full, teaspoons, or even bowls full of whatever you are using. The object is to simmer the herb in the water for 15 minutes to several hours. This depends on how strong you want this preparation to be. Simmer is different than steep. For simmer, you have the heat under the preparation on low but for steep, you pour hot water over the herb and allow it to sit, covered. One can to make a double strength preparation by straining the liquid off and adding a new batch of herbs to this already simmered product. These are generally taken as a warm tea or applied to the body warm.

In class we make a Burdock Root **Decoction**. This decoction is used at my house as a vegetarian soup base. After class is over, I add carrots, potatoes, onions and anything else that I have in the house to this decoction. What a wonderful healing stew/soup. My family never knows that they are eating a powerful blood cleanser.

Because it is such a great blood cleaner, it will clean up things like: Gout, Boils, Cancer, Abscesses, Skin diseases, Eczema, Fevers, Cold, Measles, Psoriasis, Sciatica, Tumors, Coughs, Lymphatic congestion, Rashes, Snakebite, Swelling, Tonsillitis, Acne, Allergies, Asthma, Burns, Bursitis, Canker sores, Chicken pox – internally for these problems. Externally it can be used for itching, constipation, dandruff, Herpes, Hoarseness, Impetigo, Liver problems, Lungs, Poison Ivy/Oak, Scarlet Fever, Smallpox, Sty, Water retention. All of this was referenced from Globalherb.

How can it handle all of this? According to Duke's Database, Burdock contains almost 120 ingredients. This means that when some part of the body needs something, it is available. We have allowed the body to decide what of all these things it can use to rebuild.

Burdock is a wonderful plant to have in a garden or flowerbed. I saw you do a double take just now, but it is and I will tell you why. Burdock goes 15 feet into the ground. When harvesting the root, we might be able to get

The Simplicity of Herbal Health

some of those 15 feet to use for our decoction. The rest of this root will die and leave organic matter in the soil. Burdock is a two-year plant, so even if the first year isn't harvested and allowed to grow for the second year, it will die and leave organic matter deep in the soil. OK, but what about all those burrs? The burrs only grow on a second year plant. The first year it looks like rhubarb and should not be confused with rhubarb because its root and leaves are not healthy. The second year, Burdock grows tall and puts seeds (Burrs) out. These burrs can be useful. I have been told that a tea of the burr is great for arthritis. But in my yard, I cut the seeds off from the plants. The part that makes the burrs is put into the compost pile. I leave one plant to create seeds for the next year's crop.

With all this organic matter in the soil, our angleworms are happier and our soil is alive.

Phyllis Heitkamp Master Herbalist

Blood Cleansers

Burdock is such a great blood cleanser. It is the major ingredient in Essiac Tea. Essiac is a cancer cure that was given to a nurse in Canada by the local Indians. They couldn't believe what they saw that we were doing to cure cancers. The Nurse had great success with this formula. Most Herbalists have heard of Essiac and have found it to be very helpful.

There are other blood cleansers that have been used for hundreds of years for cancers. Red Clover Blossoms were used to clean up cancer when Jethro Kloss, author of Back To Eden was growing up in Manitowoc, Wisconsin. Red Clover Blossoms are able to do all the things that Burdock can. So if one isn't available in your area, perhaps another one is?

Another blood cleanser is Chaparral. Chaparral is supposed to be one of those herbs that will kill you but in reality it can save your life. I checked in Varro Tyler's book but Chaparral isn't in there because he knows that the powers-that-be have put it on the dangerous list, the "No, No list" if you will.

According to The Little Herb Encyclopedia, Mexicans along with North American Indian tribes have been using Chaparral for centuries. It will tone up the system and rebuild tissues. It will also clean up the urethral tract and is a strong cleansing herb for the kidneys. Many universities have tested Chaparral and found it an aid in dissolving tumors and in fighting cancer. It is a strong antioxidant, painkiller and antiseptic. After 2,000 years of recorded history, after the many universities have tested the plant and have found that it aids in dissolving tumors and fighting cancer, the FDA now want to take Chaparral off the market.

Many herbalists know of the wonderful things that Chaparral is capable of doing. In The Scientific Validation of Herbal Medicine by Dr. Mowrey, I found listed in the index under Chaparral: Adrenals, Analgesic, Anti-rheumatoid, Antibacterial, Anticancer, Antimicrobial, Antioxidant, Arthritis, Ascorbic acid levels, Dental caries, Detoxify/nurture, Pain relief, Skin cancer, Skin disorders, and Vasodepressant. One of these references said that at Brooks hospital in Boston, scientists found a substance in Chaparral that inhibited the formation of dental caries (Cavities). Mowrey also states, "Chaparral has substantial clinical and experimental support as a treatment for skin cancer." He also mentions that it inhibits bacteria and molds.

The Simplicity of Herbal Health

Chaparral is hard to purchase because the powers–that-be, do not like the fact that one can go into the desert and pick a cure instead of spending thousands of dollars on chemicals or surgery or radiation. At one time it was doing such a good job that areas of the desert were sprayed with chemicals to make Chaparral unusable for healing.

There are so many ways to clean up cancer. We have just talked about three of them and they are blood cleansers. Some of the things that are talked about as cancer, Hanna Kroeger used to treat like the common cold because they are just another virus. (The medical profession is just starting to get a handle on virus) Dr. Hulda Clark, in her book <u>The Cure For All Cancers</u>, talks about finding parasites at the root of a lot of cancer.

Hanna has a book called, <u>Parasites, the Enemy Within</u>. Most of us don't want to admit that we have parasites but a great many of us do. Hanna mentioned that people who have dark circles under their eyes should be check for parasites. There are Liver Flukes. They are tiny flat worms, which undermine the health of the liver. They make holes throughout the liver causing things like: Jaundice, swelling of the liver, general poisoned condition and even pain in the right side. We talked about how to deal with parasites in Chapter I but Hanna has a vibrational remedy to handle Liver Flukes.

Hanna Kroeger felt that most cancers were attached to a fungus. She felt that it was a virus feeding on a fungus so her way of handling cancer was to get the fungus out. She mentioned that when the virus has run out of fungus to feed on, it could no longer function in the body. This is why the virus metastasizes to another area of the body from time to time, it runs out of "food" so it moves on.

When Hanna came to this country from Germany, she thought it was her gift to America to teach the cure for Leukemia. In the hospital where she worked in Dresden, Germany, they were able to clean it up in a week. According to Hanna, no one wanted to hear this, so she went on to teach about alternative health care. But she did tell us that Leukemia is not a cancer as there is no tumor. She said that emotional problems would become Leukemia. In her book she talked about how to deal with this problem. In classes she talked about the fact that our tail bone moves with every breath that we take. It pumps bone marrow to the spleen to make healthy red blood cells. Without this, she said, the red cells are weak and

Phyllis Heitkamp Master Herbalist

the white takes over. She showed the class how to reset the tailbone so it could do its job. To learn how to do this check out her book <u>God Helps Those Who Help Themselves.</u>

When she talked about Lymphoma, she suggested cleaning up the liver and getting the parasites out, mainly protozoa and Lymph flukes. The Merck Manual talks about Lymphoma and one cause is the Epstein–Barr virus. This virus can also go into Mononucleosis. Hanna has a combination for Epstein–Barr virus. She calls it the *BE Kit*. It contains three different things. The first is an herbal capsule called *A33* and it consists of Eucalyptus, Club Moss, Tarragon, Condurango Bark, and Jasmine Tea. The second herbal combination contains Raspberry leaves, Basil, and Lettuce. The third is a vibrational used by a Dr. Ray, one of Hanna's teachers, and it is called *B.E.*

My daughter was tired all the time and really run down so when we found out that she had Epstein-Barr, I wasn't surprised. I sent the kit to her and when she finished it, she called to tell me about all the energy that she had and how she was always hungry. It was nice to see her back to normal.

David Slater has continued and expanded on Hanna's work. He feels that there are many things that create tumors. With his study, he has a program that is called Lumps and Bumps. In it he has found 62 different kinds of "lumps or bumps". Connected with these could be one or more of the 19 different Retrovirus or one of the 19 Coxsackie A virus. It could be one of the 27 Coxsackie B virus or one of the 72 Papilloma virus or the Papilloma Bone virus or one of the 15 fungus that he has listed or one of the 20 blanket problems (From Adeno to Strep). It could be one of the 18 other things that he has found that will clump cells together in a tumor (from Bug Spray to Mercurous arsenic.)

* * *

Retrovirus is another problem that I would like to address here, as it is something that has been mentioned by David Slater. Retrovirus according to Hanna Kroeger in her report called, <u>Retrovirus - The Newcomer</u>, was introduced into humans through the Salk Vaccine. "This ape virus has the scientific name of Simian 40, in short Sim 40. It is a Retrovirus, an RNA virus. Sim 40 is harmless to apes, but when it entered into the bloodstream of our children the disaster started. Many physicians realized very soon

The Simplicity of Herbal Health

that something went wrong with the inoculations. Sim 40 had never been in human blood before, and all at once millions of Americans had it."

This virus was very important to Hanna because after being vaccinated Hanna's daughter was affected. Before this the child had no problems being a very normal child. Now as an adult, she will always function at the mental level of a child. But she is alive and at one time through all of this, Hanna had given her up to God because this virus was so severe.

She found out that... " 'Retro' is a prefix denoting: *at the back of or behind, backwards.* Since Retrovirus contain this unique enzyme (Reverse Transcriptase), they have the ability to copy their genetic information backwards. " Virus are too small to be seen but they operate within a host cell, while bacteria can live outside of cells. The cells that the Salk Vaccine was made in were monkey cells that contained this virus.

Hanna created an *X-40 kit* to try to handle this. The *X-40 kit* contains an herbal combination of Angelica, Calamus, Fennel, Gentian, Peppermint and Yarrow. It also contains an Indian tea, (My guess is that it is similar to Essiac Tea) and after much prayer, she added "*Sacramental Nr. 90-43*" (A vibrational to make everything work harder.) It can be used on Hepatitis C (Liver cancer), Retrovirus, and Polio.

* * *

Cholesterol

Our next subject is cholesterol and what it does to the body. Cholesterol is just one way to get high blood pressure. Did you know that high blood pressure is not a disease but the result of what we eat and how we live?

In an article called "Alternative View-Chinese Healing Practices Peak Western Interest", written by Anne Barnard of the Boston Globe, states that "A common Chinese diagnosis in patients with high blood pressure is 'liver fire rising,' which often correlates to excess anger and stress."

Cholesterol is the lubricant that keeps us flexible. When the liver is so congested with chemicals and other toxins from our present world, it stores the Cholesterol in other places like the arteries and veins. Now the blood has to wind its way through all of this junk. If the arteries or veins get completely closed off, the blood can't get to the cells that need the nutrition and we have cell-death. Being very resourceful, the body will even create new channels for this blood to use and we have varicose veins or maybe heart bypass surgery to have new channels for the blood to use.

Everyone thinks that if they have high cholesterol, they have a heart problem but they really have a liver problem. Clean up the liver and it will work for you and not against you.

In one of Hanna Kroeger's lectures she mentioned that liver hormones are made in the right shinbone. She says that if the right leg is tender, it is always a cholesterol problem. She has an herbal product called *KOLESTER*. It contains Okra, Male Fern, Beth Root, Rhubarb Root and Calamus Root. In her book, <u>God Helps Those That Help Themselves</u>, she said, "a Japanese laboratory found that in the right shinbone a special hormone is formed which is picked up by the white corpuscles and delivered to the liver to be utilized for cholesterol processing. Since in some cases this hormone is in short supply, cholesterol-triglyceride trouble starts. Here is an herbal formula which helps to create the missing hormone...." She recommends a cup of arnica and hyssop tea three times a day for this.

The first thing that the medical profession wants to do is cut the fats out of our diet. And for the most part it isn't that bad of an idea except that we need fat in our diets. So the best thing would be to cut out most of the animal fats and use only plant fats.

Every article that I see talks about cutting fats out of our diets, even vegetable fats that can be helpful and are high in Vitamin E and many trace minerals. They do tell people to cut back on meat, the animal fat is cholesterol that was made by that animal. So the liver doesn't even have to make it, we can get it in its original form.

Fats that are helpful come from plant oils such as Olive, Almond, Sesame, Primrose, Purslane, Flax, Coconut and many others. They do not contribute to this problem. I have heard that the body will not give up fat unless it has a substitute. Fat is another place that toxins are stored in the body but to get rid of these toxins, a trade must be made. Olive Oil is a great place to start. Flax Seed oil is great. I have taken a tablespoonful daily for short periods of time to help release toxic fats. Flaxseed Oil doesn't have much of a taste but I don't care for the oily residue in my mouth so I do a juice chaser after taking this. For people who don't want

The Simplicity of Herbal Health

the oily feeling at all, these oils can be found in gel caps or one can eat the Flaxseeds in their whole form.

My latest oil is that of the coconut. We will be talking about oils more in a later chapter so I won't discuss it here except to say that the body needs oils

To help break down the cholesterol that is already in the body, I suggest Lecithin. Soy is a great source of Lecithin, if you haven't tried it, now is the time. Other things that contain Lecithin are nuts such as Peanuts, Pumpkins, Brazil nuts, Hickory nuts along with Sunflower seeds and flaxseeds. Strawberries have lecithin as does Dandelion flowers. Even Plums have some lecithin.

Butcher's Broom is a wonderful herb to get the cholesterol moving in the body. What we are trying to do is break this fatty substance down and move it back to the liver to be made into bile and then sent out of the body. What Butcher's Broom does is keep the fats from sticking to the walls of the arteries and veins. When you use Butcher's Broom, your cholesterol test will show an increase because you now have all of the cholesterol loose in the blood stream. As the liver disposes of this, it will come down. People, whose tests show low blood cholesterol can have high cholesterol but it is probably attached to the walls of the veins and arteries and doesn't show up in a blood test.

Butcher's Broom is a plant that got its name from the butchers who used it in Europe. Originally it was tied into bundles and used to scrub the cutting areas in meat markets. They found that by rubbing this plant on their cutting boards and then cutting up chicken, they could clean the cutting boards easily because the fats didn't stick. It works the same way in your body.

Other herbs to stimulate the movement of cholesterol are Garlic, Cayenne, Ginseng, Parsley, Ginger and any of the blood cleansers that were mentioned in the first part of this chapter.

We take in more calcium than most people in other countries. We will be discussing this in a later chapter but for now we are concerned with the amount that is parked on the walls of our veins and arteries. This is the stuff that is creating the inflexibility or hardening of the arteries; hence, creating high blood pressure. I like to make a drink that calls for Organic

Phyllis Heitkamp Master Herbalist

Apple Cider Vinegar and water. I make this by pouring a little apple cider vinegar in a tall glass. Then adding an equal amount of honey and stir them together. Now I have about one eighth of the glass filled. I fill the rest with distilled water and add ice cubes. It is wonderful. My husband thinks this is a very refreshing drink in the summer. He doesn't know that it is also good for him.

When we want to clean the minerals off glass, we use vinegar and water. Well, we are doing the same thing inside of our bodies, we are removing the excess minerals. It does not remove the calcium that is being used by the body in teeth and bones. It uses the junk that is lining the veins and arteries or creating spurs and arthritis.

Yes, we need calcium but we need it to be organic so the body can use it. We are organic beings. Plants grow with calcium. We also need it in combination with trace minerals so that the body can readily use it. Dr. Christopher has a formula that is called *Calcium Assimilation Formula*. It contains Horsetail grass, Oat straw, Comfrey root and Lobelia. There is nothing in this formula that is high in calcium but they are all high in silica and other trace minerals that help the body utilize any calcium that is available. According to Dr. Christopher, " As explained in the book <u>Biological Transmutations</u>, the silica in horsetail grass converts to calcium, and the other herbs work in close conjunction with this master calcium herb."

Dr. Christopher suggested soaking feet in a tea made of his *Calcium Assimilation Formula,* for bone spurs. He also suggested taking the capsules of this formula for stones in the Gall or kidneys.

Bone spurs and stones are helped by drinking the apple cider vinegar and soaking in it.

* * *

When we supply the body with the building blocks to help it repair or to get the toxins out, it does a great job of healing itself. Doing a liver cleanse once a year helps the body function more efficiently. Liver cleanses also help with eye health.

The Simplicity of Herbal Health

Liver Cleans

Use the juice of 1 lemon and 1 orange.
Blend it with 2 cloves of garlic and one
Tablespoon of Olive oil.
Drink

In 30 minutes make a tea of;
1 part Comfrey
1 part Fenugreek
2 parts Peppermint.

Take daily for one week as a liver cleanse. Take as needed for a tonic
Is refreshingly effective on the liver.
Sounds weird - tastes good.

* * *

Liver Flush

Take stewed tomatoes only for 2 days
On the second night take:
3 oz. Olive Oil
2 oz. Caster Oil
3 oz. un-whipped whipping cream.

* * *

Liver Cleanse

Put the juice of 2 limes in a quart of water.
Drink 1 quart a day for 10 days.

* * *

There are many more liver cleanses to be found. Find one that you like and do it once a year to assist the liver with all the toxins that are going through there.

* * *

We haven't forgotten the gallbladder. Hanna tells us about an interesting diet for this and the liver. "I have a book from the 17th century in which an old physician from Austria gives his secrets. One of them is the

Apple Juice diet. This diet is greatly used among health minded people to detoxify liver and gall bladder. Here it is, and I recommend it to everyone very, very highly. Give your gallbladder a rest, a chance, a holiday."

First day
8 a.m. 1 glass (8 oz) Apple Juice
10 a.m. 2 glasses (8 oz) Apple Juice
12 p.m. 2 glasses (8 oz.) Apple Juice
2 p.m. 2 glasses (8 oz.) Apple Juice
4 p.m. 2 glasses (8 oz.) Apple Juice
6p.m. 2 glasses (8 oz.) Apple Juice
8 p.m. 2 glasses (8 oz.) Apple Juice
No food is to be taken this day.

Second Day

Same procedure as for the first day. No food this day either. At bedtime on the second day take 4 oz. Olive Oil. You many wash the olive oil down with hot Lemon juice or hot Apple juice.

As a rule this diet starts to work next morning. In the fecal matter you will find little green pebbles. They may be the size of a pinhead or they may be as big as a bird egg. Many times it all looks like green mud.

In any case, the old stagnant bile becomes dissolved and liquefied through the malic acid of the apple juice – which should be sugar and chemical free – and the oil moves the whole mess."

* * *

According to Hanna, there are also some cleansers for the Lymph:

Barley; Boil three tablespoons barley in one quart water for thirty minutes. Add a little clove and cinnamon. Drink this in one day, it will clear the congestion in the lymphatic system.

Or

Apple whey: Take one-pint apple juice or apple wine, one pint of water and one pint of milk. Heat it slowly but do not bring it to a boil. When it curdles, strain it through a fine cloth, throw the curds away, and sweeten with honey if needed. Take two tablespoons five times daily if the person is very weak. The appetite will come soon. As the patient gets stronger give up to two cups a day, it is powerful.

Phyllis Heitkamp Master Herbalist

Eyes and Ears

Eyes and Ears need to be fed too. When is the last time that you fed this area and yet we expect them to always work perfectly.

I have to tell a personal story here. In every class that I do, I try to show my students just how safe these preparations are that we make. In one chapter we made a skin salve. When I get to that point of this class, I take a jar of salve and dip my finger into it, then put this salve on one of my eyeballs. Usually only on the right side so I can continue to read my notes, as the oil in the salve will make my eye blurry for a time.

When I first started doing this, my eye would water and I could feel the oil sliding around the eyeball. Soon my nose would run as most of my eye problems are caused from chronic sinus problems. But I continued to do this and after a few years, I found that my right eye wasn't doing well...at least that is what I thought. It seemed that looking through my right eye, things were blurry and my left eye had to do most of the work.

Then I found out that if I take my glasses off, my left eye is blurry and my right eye can read signs and see things in sharp contrast. I joked about taking the lens out of the right side of my glasses but instead, I have decided only to use my glasses to read. This way I will be exercising both of them.

What was I doing to my right eye? I was giving it nutrition that it isn't getting in the normal fashion. Dr. Christopher kept repeating that there is only one disease and that is constipation/congestion. When the cells are not getting the nutrition or able to get the toxins out, we have a problem.

Dr. Christopher has an eyewash product called *Herbal Eyebright Formula*. It contains Eyebright, Bayberry bark, Goldenseal Root, Red Raspberry leaves and Cayenne. It is in a tincture form and this is dropped into an eyecup that is full of boiling hot water. This hot water is necessary to dissipate the alcohol in the tincture. When it has cooled, the eyecup is put to the eye and then the eye is moved in as many directions as possible, allowing this herbal formula to go all over the eye. Most people have a problem with this formula because it contains Capsicum, and therefore stings the eyeball. It doesn't burn the eye but draws the blood to this area to get the circulation going and bring nutrition to it. When people are starting

The Simplicity of Herbal Health

with this product, they usually can not open their eyes but do it through the lid. It is a powerful formula but when it is the difference between seeing and not seeing, people will do anything.

People using Dr. Christopher's eyewash formula have gotten rid of cataracts and glaucoma. It has been used to clean up an eye puncture and has opened tear ducts.

In combination with other formulas such as; the *Ear & Nerve Formula* (formerly called B&B formula) and the *Complete Tissue Formula* (Formerly the Bones, Flesh and Cartilage formula), people have been able to handle maligned eye retina problems and even Dyslexia.

Dr. Christopher talked about a baby who was born without an optic nerve and by using the nerve formula along with Eye Bright, within 6 months this child could follow a ball. He conditioned this with the need for Love, proper food, and herbs.

The Christopher School of Natural teaches a class on Iridology. This is the study of looking at the iris of the eye and being able to tell what is happening in the body. For example; if there is a black line in the iris at the 12 o'clock area, the animation lifeline is in malfunction. It means that you need to have someone get you moving. It is a whole study of which I did not partake so I can't elaborate more on it. But when you clean up the body, you clean up the eyes.

Dr. Christopher mentioned that he has seen eyes go from brown to blue after the body has been cleansed of all the toxins that where there.

My father-in-law, Earl wanted something to work on his eyes so I suggested Bilberry capsules to him. They are usually standardized for the anthocyanidin compound in them. I am very much against standardizing so I wrote to Dr. Duke regarding the necessity of standardizing herbs. I have expressed my feelings about this in another area of this book so I will say that Dr. Duke told me that Bilberry isn't the only berry to contain this helpful nutrient for the eyes. He suggested that Blueberries, Black Berries, Black Cherries and even Chokecherries are high in anthocyanidin. Some are even found free in many areas of the country.

Chickweed is soothing and mild, and it will take the red out of the eyeball. It will pull the toxin out of a sty.

Phyllis Heitkamp Master Herbalist

Hanna Kroeger has a lot of remedies in her book <u>Heal Your Life with Home Remedies and Herbs.</u> One is that Cardamom is eye and brain food. Others are Angelica root tea, Fennel as an eyewash, Maple syrup, Rosemary, Linden flower tea, Sunflowers seeds, all help strengthen the eyes. She has suggestions in this book on cataracts, optic nerve problems, farsightedness, and inflammation of the eyes, retinal bleeding, twitching eyelid, and much more.

She has mentioned that if the skin is dark under the eye, parasites might be the problem. In regard to parasites, Toxoplasosis is the single cell parasite that is found in cat feces that will affect the eyes of an unborn child. I have cats and did the cure for this parasite. When one takes this cure, one must also cure their cats of this too. My cats got sick from the cure. They ran a fever for one day and then all was well.

Hanna also suggests that glaucoma can come from congestion of the pancreas. Her cure for Cataracts is: 1 quart of distilled water, dissolve 6 level tablespoons of Cream of Tarter in the water along with 2 tablespoons of Borax. Using a wash cloth saturated in this solution, place on the eye. I have never tried this so if anyone does, I would like to hear the results.

* * *

Our next topic is about ears. Here is an area of the body that needs some attention. We all take hearing for granted until we start to have a problem with it.

Sometimes helping the ears helps the eyes too. The ears have a lot of nerves in them and they are the closest things to the optic nerve, so we have found that by feeding the ears with nervines, one can help both of them. The *Ear and Nerve Formula* that was discussed earlier is a great formula for using in the ear canal. A warning here, never put anything in the ear canal if the eardrum has been punctured. If the eardrum is intact, apply some drops of the *Ear and Nerve Formula* to nourish the nerves of the inner ear. Dr. Christopher told us a story of how a grandfather got rid of his hearing aids after using this formula.

With humming or sounds in the ear (Tinnitus), one might want to use Club Moss tincture. Dr. Christopher suggests using Garlic oil and the *Ear and Nerve Formula* for this problem also.

The Simplicity of Herbal Health

Tinnitus could be coming from calcification in the inner ear and Apple Cider Vinegar in water might be helpful for this too. One could drink it along with using it in the ear canal.

Hanna talked about earaches and how some of Children's earaches are related to psychological problems such as loneliness or homesickness or even fear. For this she suggests having the child's crib put into the parent's room for a period of time or putting fur next to the child in a car seat.

For adults with earaches, Hanna suggests checking for a Candida problem, or putting a poultice of cinnamon, cloves and sassafras behind the ear. Another suggestion was to use 6 drops of a tincture made from the Chicks & Hens plant. Another suggestion that she has is to eat asparagus to help with ear problems and rubbing down both sides of the neck from the back of the ear to the collarbone to open the Eustachian tube.

An onion sliced and put behind the ear is said to soften earwax.

Hanna suggested putting Sassafras oil on the "tough" skin on the palm of the hand and cupping them over the ear. A lady that I knew tried this on her grandson's ears. He was supposed to have ear tubes put in soon. That was averted.

Other things that have been attributed to ear problems have to do with the drinking of milk from a bottle. As we talked about earlier, dairy makes mucus and if this mucus tends to back up into the eustachian tube, the inner ear can get clogged up.

The ear canal is a nice place for fungus and there are many things that can be used for this. I like to use Black Walnut tincture for its anti-fungal properties but garlic oil works well for this too.

Mullein ear oil, made from the flowers of the Mullein can be used to nourish and cleanse the ears.

I have a note that I want to pass on about ear candles. These are cones that are made of a cloth material that has been waxed and formed into a long cone shape. The small end is supposed to be inserted into the outer ear and the end that is about 10 to 15 inches from the head is then lighted. The flame is put out and the cone tends to smolder, with a smoke

Phyllis Heitkamp Master Herbalist

rising. The intended purpose is to "pull" wax and other things out of the ear with this up draft. Hanna thinks that ear candles should be used in another manner. Her suggestion is that one candle a week should be used in the navel to pull negative emotions out of the body. I will have to agree with her but I have had some people tell me how beneficial an ear candle treatment has been for them.

The Simplicity of Herbal Health

Where Do We Start?

So where do we start with our herbal health? We start by eating good food and herbs. Remember, Dr. Christopher said that we need 5 things to keep us healthy, (The mucusless diet) Fruits, Vegetables, Whole grains, Nuts and Seeds.

We need to clean up the intestinal system so that when the liver cleans out, the toxins have a way to get out.

We need to keep the liver healthy

We need to exercise and keep the body moving.

Dr. Christopher told us there is only one dis-ease and that is constipation/congestion. By cleaning out the liver and the G.I tract, we can begin to see our health improve.

As homework for this chapter, I would like to suggest making a decoction if you will. As you travel through this text, I am hoping you will want to try to make some of the herbal preparations so when and if you need them, you will know how to process them.

Keep a record of how you do this so you can repeat or alter it as you need to.

Have fun and remember nature is wonderful. The Bible talks about the fruit of the tree being used for food and the leaves for medicine.

Chapter II - Resources

Atkins, Robert C., MD, *Dr. Atkins' Vita-nutrient Solution,* Fireside, NY, 1998, 407 pg.

Blake, Steven, <u>Global Herb-Computer program</u> - *Version 3.0,* California, 1995

Challem, J., Berkson, Burt, and Smith, Melissa, Diane, *Syndrome X – The Complete Nutritional Program To Prevent And Reverse Insulin Resistance,* 2000, John Wiley & Sons, NY., 272 pg.

Christopher, David, M.H. & Fawn, *A Healthier You – Audio Newsletter,* Christopher Publications, Springville, Utah, 1999, 1-800-372-8255

Christopher, John R., Dr., *School of Natural Healing,* Christopher Publications, Springville, Utah, 1976, 724 pg., <u>www.snh.cc</u>

Christopher, John R., ND., MH., *Dr. Christophter's Three-Day Cleansing Program, Mucusless Diet and Herbal Combinations,* Christopher Publications, Inc., Springville, UT. 1969, 34 pg. ,<u>www.snh.cc</u>

Clark, Hulda R., Ph.D., ND, *The Cure for all Cancers,* New Century Press, San Diego, CA. 1995, 590 pg.

Duke, James A., Ph.D., <u>*Dr. Duke's Phytochemical and Ethnobotanical Database*</u>, 2003

Reprinted with permission from *Back To Eden* by Jethro Kloss, Lotus Press, PO Box 325, Twin Lakes, WI 53181. © 1999 All Rights Reserved.

Kroeger, Hanna, Rev., *God Helps Those That Help Themselves,* 1984

Kroeger, Hanna, Rev., *Retro-Virus - The Newcomer,* 1992, Report

Kroeger, Hanna, Rev., *Heal Your Live with Home Remedies and Herbs,* Hay House, Inc., Carlsbad, CA, 1998, 296 pg.

From *The Merck Manuel of Medical Information – Home Edition,* P. 1509, edited by Mark H Beers and Robert Berkow, Copyright 1997 by Merck & Co., Inc., Whitehouse Station, NJ.

Mowrey, Daniel B. Ph.D., *The Scientific Validation of Herbal Medicine,* Keats Publishing, Inc., New Canaan, CT., 1986, 316 pg.

Ritchason, Jack, ND., *The Little Herb Encyclopedia,* Woodland Health Books, Pleasant Grove, Utah, 1995, 402 pg.

Slater, David, <u>Healers Who Share</u>, Westminster, Co. 2000

Chapter III
Tea of the Day

We are ready to make another infusion to start this chapter.

Red Clover blossoms are wonderful and make a nice tasting tea. When you eat the fresh blossom, you understand why bumblebees like it. There is a sweet taste found at the base of the petals.

I was talking to a middle-aged lady about eating blossoms and she mentioned that she used to eat Red Clover Blossoms all the time as a child. When I told her how wonderful they were and what they did, she was surprised. I think most of us do not know what is growing around us that is there for our health. My sister tells people that I "graze" in my yard and she is right. A nibble here and a nibble there, maybe I don't get a full meal out of my yard but when I think of all the constituents each thing I nibble on is giving me, I know that I am doing some good for this body. I am giving my body 120 different things to chose from when I eat Red Clover Blossoms according to Duke's Database. He states there is everything in this plant from Beta-carotene to Salicylic acid.

If that were all one found in Red Clover tea, it would be nice but this little blossom is a "heavy duty" herb. It has been used for hundreds of years to handle cancers, breast as well as bowel, according to John Heinerman in his book <u>Science Of Herbal Medicine</u>; and the Lloydia Survey done in '67-'71 called <u>Plants Used Against Cancer</u>; then again found in <u>Back To Eden</u> by Jethro Kloss.

According to the Globalherb computer program, it works well for bronchitis, sores, coughs, even whooping cough and many more things. This is because of its ability to act as a blood cleanser in the body. What does a blood cleanser do? It helps the cells release stored toxins that are in the system, to clean and flush them out of the body.

The Simplicity of Herbal Health

The Heart

According to Hanna Kroeger, some of us have a genetic heart problem that she calls a Miasma. This means that it has been handed down from generation to generation. When this happens, it takes a little longer to clean it up. Did you know that every organ could rebuild if 10% of that organ is healthy and you start to supply it with the right nutrition?

Hanna has an herbal combination called *Heartwarmer,* for healing the heart. The main stay of this combination is Hawthorn Berry but it also contains Chickweed, Motherwort, Capsicum and Cramp bark. All great herbs by themselves but when put into this combination, they work wonders.

Hawthorn Berry is used extensively in Europe for heart conditions. Hawthorn is used as a tonic, which means that it is usually taken over a long period of time to get the results desired.

Hawthorn dilated vessels away from the heart, there-by increasing blood flow to the heart. It increases the "enzyme metabolism in the heart muscle" according to Daniel B. Mowrey in his book, The Scientific Validation of Herbal Medicine. It increases the oxygen used by the heart.

In my book, Wisconsin Medicinal Herbs, I wrote over three pages of all the wonderful things that Hawthorn is capable of doing.

Some of the things that Hawthorn Berry is capable of doing according to the Globalherb program are: act as a digestive aid, handle blood clots, handle general swelling, and it is even good for a sore throat

Dr. Christopher says that Hawthorn Berry is a cardiac food. He suggested using Cayenne or Hawthorn Berries after a heart attack until that area can be rebuilt. He said that heart conditions could come from 100 different causes so giving the body cardiac food sure sounds like a good idea to me.

Note here: Cayenne is supposed to balance out the blood pressure in the whole body so that one area is not dealing with more than another. Dr. Christopher suggested that if someone was in the process of having a heart attack, sipping on water with cayenne in it, might help to stabilize that person and assist by minimizing the damage done.

Hawthorn grows as a tree, from 15 to 30 feet tall. There are as many as 1000 species in North America. When you find a Hawthorn, you will know it because it has long, two to three inch spike-like thorns on it branches.

The fruit resembles a miniature apple but it has two large seeds in relationship to its pea-sized fruit. It should resemble an apple, as it belongs to the Rose family along with Apples, Apricots, Quince, Wild Cherries, Raspberries and Blackberries.

Let me tell you how Hawthorn works on the heart muscle. The heart muscle needs Calcium, Potassium and Magnesium. Hawthorn Berries are very high in the first two and sufficiently high in the third one. Hawthorn also has Chromium, which is said to lower the bad cholesterol (LDL) and raise the good cholesterol (HDL). Hanna Kroeger mentioned that in China, they studied it and said that it would lower cholesterol along with triglycerides.

As you found out in the last chapter, the heart doesn't make cholesterol but has to deal with it, so if you are dealing with cholesterol or triglycerides perhaps you need to go back a chapter and find out how to make the Liver work properly?

Hawthorn also contains Selenium, which strengthens weak hearts. Selenium is very hard to find in our food supply but Hawthorn being a tree, has roots down 15 to 30 feet in the ground. Trees are able to find trace minerals by stretching out their hair roots until they find them. Trace minerals are just that. We need traces of some of these things. We do not need a whole capsule of Selenium. When we look at the percentage of some of these trace minerals, we find .00029% of something. This small amount will assist all the other things to do their job of creating a balance. Herbs have trace minerals.

Hawthorn, like its cousin the Apple, is very high in Vitamin C. When we combine Vitamin C with Selenium, we have two of the most important antioxidants in the nutritional world. This combination is said to protect against strokes. Vitamin C is very good at protecting the arteries against capillary breakage or leakage along with excessive clotting. Vitamin C also helps to lower cholesterol levels.

What we are doing when we use Hawthorn Berries is supplying the heart with all the elements that nourish it. Now the heart muscle can rebuild. One can not make a cake without flour and eggs in the house. The body is losing cells everyday and if it isn't being supplied with the building blocks to rebuild, we are in trouble.

Hanna Kroeger mentioned that Hawthorn would not work like digitalis does, as it doesn't contain the same compounds. There are many herbs that have different properties but accomplish what is called for in this area. She also had great success with Blue Malva Tea to heal heart valves. We will be talking about the Malva family later in this book. In Germany, Hawthorn is used as a tonic for the elderly whether or not they have a heart condition.

Dr. Shen, a Chinese Herbalist that I met on the Internet, had a drink that he suggested for recovery from by-pass surgery. His formula was: Chinese sage (dan shen) 9 gm, Safflower (hong hua) 9 gm, Pseudoginseng root (san qi) 3 gm, and Chinese licorice root (zhi gan cao) 6 gm. Slow boil the herbs in 4 cups of water for 40 minutes. Drink twice a day along with Hawthorn and Ginseng.

Phyllis Heitkamp Master Herbalist

Making a Tonic

Let's learn how to make a **tonic**. To make a Hawthorn Berry **tonic**, the berries are soaked if we are dealing with a dried product. Then we simmer them for 20 to 30 minutes, using the water that we soaked them in, strain and return the liquid to a cleaned kettle. Next, we add raw sugar (Sucanat- Sugar Cane Natural) as a preservative. We will be talking about the different sugars later in this chapter. Now we allow it to cool, and bottle it. This is good for many months in the refrigerator. Sometimes I like to add a little Black Cherry Juice Concentrate for flavor but Hawthorn has a very nice taste by itself.

While making the tonic, we might notice the dark red/purple color in our product. This compound is known as flavonoids. Hawthorn Berries have a large amount of this substance, which is said to balance the body's hormones. "Flavonoids work with Vitamin C (Hawthorn being high in Vitamin C) to build bones, collagen, tendons, capillaries and strong teeth," states Hanna Kroeger. Here are the additional bonuses that we need. Flavonoids are found in all the dark-skinned berries. Even the French like red wine for this reason...a healthy heart.

Dr. Atkins calls bioflavonoids the "first family of Antioxidants". He mentioned that "flavoniods in general, but quercetin in particular, may be more potent than vitamin E for disarming cholesterol's potential threat to the heart. A high intake of the nutrient corresponds to a significantly lower risk of cardiovascular disease and stroke." This is all according to several large studies that have been done. Dr. Atkins has called Quercetin the "king of the Flavonoids". He mentioned that briefly in the 1920s we had a vitamin P and then it was reclassified as nonessential but the good doctor feels that we can not "spell health without it", so Flavonoids are essential to good health. Vitamin P is said to feed the capillaries and the brain. This "King" keeps the blood from thickening and forming clots. It keeps the LDL cholesterol from oxidation or turning rancid. Quercetin can also be found in Green Tea, Red wine, Apples, Onions, Green Peppers, Tomatoes, and Broccoli.

Hawthorn is usually made into a **tonic** and taken daily over a long period of time to get the results that have been mentioned here. I have found that when my upper left arm is giving me trouble (Discomfort), I can

The Simplicity of Herbal Health

take a Hawthorn Berry capsule or its tonic and the "trouble" dissipates in short order.

There are many other herbs that affect the heart and we will talk about some of them but none so effective, mild and safe as Hawthorn berries; yet most North American doctors are unfamiliar with it.

* * *

The next herb that I would like to discuss is Motherwort. According to Dr. Mowrey, Motherwort is found all over the world. He says that it is called "Heart wort, heart gold, heart heal or heart herb" because people recognize its use as a cardiac herb. Dr. Mowrey attributes this to its glycoside content. Everyone agrees that Motherwort has the ability to normalize heart function as it calms palpitations. Dr. Mowrey also tells us, "Recently, Motherwort extract was shown to inhibit myocardial cells, improve mesenteric circulation and increase coronary perfusion, in other words, to improve several aspect of coronary health."

This plant could be in anyone's garden but it needs to be watched as it needs no care, therefore it tends to spread seeds everywhere.

It also can be made into a **tonic** as described for Hawthorn and used not only for the heart but to calm the system and create order. Culpepper, the great herbalist, is quoted as saying "Venus owns this herb and it is under Leo. There is not a better herb to drive melancholy vapours from the heart, to strengthen it and make the mind cheerful, blithe and merry."

Many of these herbs have multiple purposes and are good at them all. This is because they contain a great many constituents, as opposed to drugs that have only the properties that will handle the situation they are targeted for.

Dr. James Duke has identified almost 50 constituents in Motherwort - some of which have the ability to be: antitumor, antioxidant, antibacterial, antiviral, and antiarrhythmic. Combined with the rest of the properties in this herb, they have the ability to assist our bodies in marvelous ways.

Motherwort tends to handle problems in other organs also such as the eyes, gall bladder, generative organs and the nervous system.

In regard to the generative organs (after all, it is called Motherwort) it is great to assist when the problem is delayed menses or stopped menses and even postpartum depression. It also would be helpful for cramps and fertility issues.

* * *

Dr. Christopher tells us that Sassafras is a wonderful herb for the heart and the circulation. Sassafras contains safro and other trace minerals that are wonderful. Safro should never been taken alone but used in the wholesome state of Sassafras. It is a blood thinner and for this reason it should not be used for longer than 6 weeks at a time but it steps up the circulation and makes the "heart sound" according to Dr. Christopher.

It is a blood purifier as it cuts cholesterol and gives elasticity to not only the heart but also the arteries and veins. Again, only in its wholesome state!

Sassafras will tackle a lot of other things such as bronchitis, flu, tobacco poisoning, ulcers, acne, it will even tackle cancer, gangrene and gout.

Other herbs that are great for the heart are: Black Cohosh, Blessed Thistle, Cayenne, Cinnamon, Cloves, Elecampane, Garlic, Ginger, Golden Seal, Licorice, Peppermint, Nutmeg, Raisins, Sage, Scullcap, Valerian, Vervain, Wood Betony, Chicory, and Reishi mushroom.

In China, Astragalus is used for the heart. The Doctors there have found that it reduces damage to heart cells and it has been known to destroy Coxsackie B Virus. Here is a virus that has been associated with heart problems and irregular heartbeats. (We will be bumping into astragalus again in this book so I will not elaborate on it here.)

Another virus that causes problems for the heart is Herpes Simplex Virus type 1. One of the herbs most used for this virus is Melissa or Lemon Balm as it is commonly called.

Ginseng is said to relieve angina spasms and pain in the heart, while Ginkgo increases the circulation as a vasodilator.

Here are two that can be used, but unless you know what you are doing, I would not advise tackling them, they are Lily of the Valley and Foxglove.

The Simplicity of Herbal Health

People often ask if they can take herbs if they are on a medication. Robert Rountree, M.D. wrote an article called <u>Herbs for Health</u>, November/December 1999, pages 28-29. In it he wrote, "So here's the question: Is it safe for a person taking digoxin to also take hawthorn? According to several recent pharmaceutical publications, the answer is either 'no' or 'with caution.' The substances have potentially additive effects, reports say. In other words, hawthorn could enhance the activity and toxicity of digoxin, requiring an adjustment in dosage. If you follow this line of reasoning, and if researchers are right about flavonoids being the active chemical in hawthorn, then patients taking digoxin should also stop eating blueberries and similar foods.

Many herbalists who agree that Hawthorn may enhance the effect of digoxin still disagree that taking hawthorn and digoxin simultaneously is dangerous. They argue the combination may actually be beneficial because the addition of Hawthorn, which is nontoxic, may make it possible to reduce the digoxin dose, which is potentially toxic."

One of the more recent finds by the medical profession is Lycopene. The drug companies are rushing to include this in their multi-vitamins. Lycopene is found in tomatoes and is most usable in cooked tomato products. One of the articles said that what Lycopene will do is to slow the process known as 'oxidative stress' said to be the main culprit in heart disease, cancer and aging. It is also found in pink grapefruit.

It is believed that the high amount of Carotenoids is what works the magic. Even the National Cancer Institute is recommending a diet high in carotenoid fruits and vegetables as they have found it to be helpful for reducing prostate cancer risk, cervical cancer, and age-related macular degenerating. But then we always knew that carrots were good for our eyes.

Isn't it wonderful when these major health organizations recognize the importance of good foods in our diet?

* * *

I have been hearing a lot about homocysteine which is an amino acid normally found in our bodies. (Amino acids are made from the protein that we digest)

Phyllis Heitkamp Master Herbalist

When we have high levels of this amino acid, researchers believe that the tissue lining of the arteries gets thick and even scars. Cholesterol will build up on the scarred tissue, clogging the passageways and creating blood clots. Homocysteine is also linked with Alzheimer's. One way to clean up the excess of this amino acid is with Vitamin B. Vitamin B is found in leafy greens. So we are back to our diet. We are eating more proteins than are needed and fewer vegetables.

Remember the five things that Dr. Christopher said we needed to stay healthy? Fruits, Vegetables, Whole Grains, Nuts and Seeds.

* * *

Hanna Kroeger talked about three metals that go to the heart and create problems. Nitrite is one of them. It is found in water, hot dogs, beef and on most vegetables as fertilizers contain this. It causes the heart to flutter. Hanna has an herbal combination called *Chem X* that contains Black Tea, Condurango Bark, Red Clover, Yellow Dock, Paprika, Chaparral, and Spikenard. She also suggests using a product made by DynaPro called *NIT*.

Another metal that goes to the heart area is Graphite. This is found in paints and lubricants. She has a vibrational that will negate Graphite and it is known by its own name.

The third one that can create problems for the heart is Cadmium. With this one, Hanna suggests that we add zinc (see list of foods high in zinc in Chapter I, Zone I) and Paprika to our diets to help with this. She also has a vibrational called *Cadmium Sulph* to help with this problem. Cadmium can create a loss of smell in the body by interrupting the signals from the olfactory nerves to the brain. It can be found in dentures, printed matter and dyes in clothing.

* * *

With regard to heart problems, Hanna tells us that we should never allow a heart that is already in trouble, do a treadmill. She says that if we are having pain in our left shoulder to the little finger, we have a heart problem but if the pain is in the right shoulder, we need to see a chiropractor first. She created a formula for heart congestion called *Circu Flow*. It contains

The Simplicity of Herbal Health

Hawthorn Berries, Equisetum concentrate, Vitamin C, Taurine, Arginine, Chromium Picolinate, Selenium. When she first made this formula, I didn't like it…Well, I am still on the fence about it because it contains so many "part-some" things in it but it is better than it used to be. This formula does not clean out cholesterol but does get the circulation going.

On a spiritual level, and we are not just physical beings, Grief and Sorrow can cause heart problems too.

Did you know that almonds are very good for the heart? Seeds are very powerful foods.

* * *

Phyllis Heitkamp Master Herbalist

Sugars

We made a **tonic** with Hawthorn berries and have used SUCANUT as the preservative. We need to talk about sugars because they are wonderful at preservation. Sucanut stands for Sugar Cane Natural. This means that the juice that was pressed out of the sugar cane was not processed but dried, leaving all the minerals and other properties intact to a large degree. Did you know that the sugar cane root go 15 feet into the soil?

The next sweetener that will be discussed is Molasses. When I speak of Molasses, please know that I am talking about Black Strap Molasses that does not have sulfur in it, nor has it been refined. It is the same as the Sucanut except it is not dried.

Molasses is the juice of the sugar cane also.

Because of the high mineral content of Natural Sugar Cane in either form, it is good for Tumors and Cancers according David Christopher. He mentions in his audio program that it is good for all kinds of things including Growths (Uterine), Strokes, Arthritis, and Ulcers (He says that it is better than Slippery Elm and Licorice for this). It is good for Skin problems (He mentions that by soaking in a diluted amount, one can get rid of dermatitis in 6 weeks.), High Blood Pressure, Constipation and Colon problems (Using it as an enema), along with Varicose Veins. That seems too good to be true but David tells us that it all happens because Black Strap Molasses contains so many things that the body needs to stay or get healthy.

He went on to talk about how rich it is in iron and therefore great for Anemia. Not just for people who have low blood iron but for people who have blood that is so poor it will not hold iron. By building up the blood it will begin to hold iron again.

David mentioned that it was great for bladder problems as well as gall stones and here is where one would add a little olive oil to the molasses.

It is helpful for nerve problems and David used the example of battle fatigue.

It is wonderful for pregnant women because it contains the basis building blocks to build a baby.

The Simplicity of Herbal Health

But Molasses is also wonderful for women who are in menopause because it has the basic building blocks to help make hormones.

It will repair hair and nails and preserve the teeth. Not the fact that it is a sugar but the fact that it is such a complete food for the body. It can be used as a mouthwash for pyorrhea. (Gum dis-ease)

Molasses is high in B vitamins and potassium, 9% of it is minerals and vitamins. This is high for a single food.

It has a germicide that destroys harmful bacteria in the intestinal tract.

It is an alkaline food, where refined sugar is an acid food. The body functions better when a bit alkaline.

Doctors say that sugar, honey and molasses are assimilated the same way but David Christopher, director of the School of Natural Healing, says that this is not so.

The next sweetener that I want to look at is Gymnema. What I learned about Gymnema leaf was that it acts as a sugar blocker with the gymnemic acid being almost identical to sugar in structure. So it locks up sugar receptors in the colon to block the sugar's absorption for about 2 hours. This information comes from a journal that one of my on-line herbalists has read. I have tried to find it but have not been able to locate it. For those of you that are reading this, understand this information is hearsay. But this plant is so important that I did find it in my Globalherb computer program, I will give you the facts that I got from there on Gymnema Leaf.

According to Globalherb, Gymnema Leaf has the actions of being a "Sugar blocker" and it "Breaks down fats. It works in the "digestion" and the "Pancreas" areas. The conditions that it handles are Appetite control, Blood sugar problems, Fat Metabolism, Obesity, Sugar craving and Weight loss.

Another sweetener that I enjoy is Stevia. Here is a plant that I grow in a pot. It is of the composite family. Dr. Bertoni "officially" discovered it in the late 19th century. He names it Stevia Rebaudi Bertoni in honor of a Paraguayan chemist. The Guarani Indians had been using the leaves of this plant to sweeten bitter teas and as a sweet treat. It is estimated that there are over 80 species of Stevia known to grow wild in North America and maybe 200 in South America.

The sweet property comes from a complex molecule called stevioside which is a glycoside made up of three things. In its natural form it is about 10 to 15 times sweeter than common table sugar. After a meal at our house, one or two leaves can be dessert.

It was found that Stevia does not affect blood sugar metabolism according to most experts. Some studies even report that Stevia may reduce plasma glucose levels in normal adults.

Okay! So what is so great about this plant? It is sugarless with no calories, will not affect blood sugar levels like sugar does, 100% natural and even sweeter than sugar, non-fermentable, flavor enhancer, recommended for diabetics. It can even be used for people with yeast infections, hypoglycemia and other conditions. I guess that is enough.

But there is even more: It has nutritional value. It contains Proteins, Fiber, Vitamin A and C, Zinc, Calcium, Phosphorus, Magnesium, Chromium and much more.

Stevia has no aftertaste in the wholesome state but my classes have tasted processed Stevia and they have not been happy with that.

It has been tested and re-tested for safety for human and animal consumption and passed with flying colors.

I hate to end this wonderful segment about sweeteners on a sour note but I am going to because I think everyone needs to be warned about the "miracle sweetener" called NUTRASWEET or Aspartame. This is a POISON. It can cause brain tumors and other cancers, along with things like Diabetes, Hearing loss, Headaches, and Dizziness. Well, I could go on and on but I will just refer you to a book called <u>Is Aspartame Safe</u> By Dr. H. J. Roberts. The product should be labeled Chemical Poison: Keep out of reach of Humans! Genocidal! Yet it is found in a lot of our foods.

The American Diabetic Association recommends it for diabetes. I wrote to them asking why and they sent me a letter stating:

The Simplicity of Herbal Health

" Dear Oakwelherb:
Re: Aspartame

There continues to be unsubstantiated claims that the non-nutritive sweetener aspartame (brand name NutraSweet) poses health risks to people with diabetes. Aspartame has been approved by the Food and Drug Administration (FDA), a governmental agency that conducts thorough scientific reviews to determine foods that are safe for public consumption.

The American Diabetes Association follows FDA recommendations and recognizes that there is no credible scientific evidence linking aspartame to any health-related problems for people with diabetes.

For all food additives, including nonnutritive sweeteners, the FDA determines an acceptable daily intake (ADI), which is defined as the amount of a food additive that can be safely consumed on a daily basis over a person's lifetime without any adverse effect, and includes a 100-fold safety factor. Actual intake of all nonnutritive sweeteners, including aspartame, is well below the ADI and therefore does not pose health risks.

The American Diabetes Association considers aspartame as well as the other FDA-approved nonnutritive sweeteners saccharin, acesulfame K, and sucralose acceptable sugar substitutes and a safe part of a diabetic meal plan.

Sincerely,

Denise Brown
Diabetes Information Representative
American Diabetes Association
National Call Center
www.diabetes.org
1-800-342-2383"

Well, there you have it. This is a planet of choice and now it is up to you to choose.

Phyllis Heitkamp Master Herbalist

High Blood Pressure

This next subject is very interesting. We are going to talk about High Blood Pressure. According to David Christopher, director of the School of Natural Healing in Springville, Utah; High blood pressure is not a disease but is the symptom of a condition. It is caused because of our lifestyle. We are clogging up our veins and arteries with waste matter and cholesterol due to our environment and our eating habits. We can reverse high blood pressure by cleaning up this body.

The drugs that are used to assist or alleviate this problem are only making it worse. One of the things that is used is a diuretic. This forces the body to excrete water. As you remember, the body needs water. So the thinking about this is that if the liquid is low in the body, the blood will be cut in half and this will get rid of the excessive pressure in the arteries. Sounds good but if you have cut the blood supply, how do the extremities get nutrition?

Another thing that is used by the medical profession is a Beta-Blocker. Beta-Blockers cut the signal that the brain is giving to the central nervous system. The brain isn't getting the nutrition that it needs so it sends a signal that tells the body to raise the pressure to make sure that the brain is getting fed. If the signal is cut, what do you think will happen? The brain, along with other areas of the body starve.

I asked a friend what kind of medication he is taking for his High Blood Pressure and he told me that it wasn't for HBP but for hypertension. This is not unusual. A lot of people do not know what they are taking medication for, if the doctor told them to take it, they take it.

I have been reading Dr. Robert C Atkins' book called <u>Vita-Nutrients Solution</u>. In it he talks about how, when he graduated from medical school, he believed everything that he was taught. But when he found his "Diet" (And he said that he found this diet in the '60's in JAMA, the Journal of American Medical Association) because he was very over-weight; he wanted to tell the world about it. So when he wrote his paper stating that he had helped thousands of people lose weight, the AMA said that they would check his facts and report their findings. According to Dr. Atkins, no one came to check his facts or interview any of the people that he had helped, but the AMA put out a report that his diet was bad. So Dr. Atkins,

The Simplicity of Herbal Health

from that day on, started doing his own research on everything the AMA said, not believing them on most subjects. The reason that I have written his history here is because I would like to use a lot of his quotes and would like the reader to understand why. He said something like, if your doctor ✱ won't suggest alternatives, get a new doctor.

Back to high Blood pressure. How do we clean up the body and get rid of HBP? We clean up the intestines so the way is made clear to get all the stuff out that is clogging up your pipes and then we heal the liver. Remember what we said in the last chapter about the liver...bitter is better.

What if nothing is clogging up the pipes but the arteries are calcified or stiff and are not flexible. We take a lot of Calcium, we take in more calcium than we need and it isn't always the right kind or even accompanied by the trace minerals that make it useable. Vitamin companies have combined calcium with magnesium, and some have even added folic acid to this combination but that isn't going to help. Our food is lacking a lot of trace minerals as the farmer only puts three things on the field; pot ash, phosphorus, and nitrogen. And for the most part this is put on in petrochemical form.

We can help our bodies absorb/utilize calcium by taking in different nutrients and varying our diet. We can do this by eating organically grown foods and taking wildcrafted herbs (Which are high in trace elements.) Some of the herbs that help move the calcium off the inside of the veins are Horsetail, Oat straw, Lobelia and Comfrey. We will talk more about these herbs in another chapter. These herbs are especially effective when used with Apple Cider Vinegar. We use organic, unfiltered Apple Cider Vinegar, the kind that has the "mother" in it. This means that some of the Apple is still in the bottle and has settled at the bottom.

One of our favorite summer drinks is Apple Cider Vinegar with honey. I put one-sixteenth of a cup of organic Apple Cider Vinegar in a tall glass. [one tablespoon] Then I add an equal amount of honey. Stir them together (they are hard to mix), then add water and ice cubes to fill the glass. It is a great alternative to lemonade and it is moving the calcium off the walls of the arteries as well.

To remove bone spurs, put Apple Cider Vinegar in water and soak the afflicted area.

81

While we are working on getting the cholesterol out of the body and we have it moving toward the liver to be emulsified and gotten rid of, our blood cholesterol level will go up. It is actually a good sign for the cholesterol levels to rise during a cleanse. It will upset your doctor and he will want to increase your medication and tell you not to take the herbs that you are taking. When the cholesterol is stuck to the walls of the arteries, your blood cholesterol levels might show that you have no cholesterol.

The herbs that are great for moving cholesterol out of the body are garlic, cayenne, parsley and ginger. The three blood cleansers are also helpful for moving the cholesterol; burdock, chaparral, and red clover.

If you are already on medication for hypertension **NEVER STOP TAKING YOUR MEDICATION SUDDENLY**. The medication messes with your brain's signals and going off a blood pressure medication is dangerous. When the brain's signals are no longer blocked, the body will find that the brain has been shouting for a long time to get nutrition. In answer to these shouts, the pressure will rise high, fast and a stroke or aneurysm could become the problem. As you clean out the system, your medical provider will start to change the dosage to a lower amount until you no longer need it.

We cleanse and nourish the body and it will heal itself.

* * *

I would be remiss if I didn't mention the problem the heart has that no one wants to talk about, Parasites. Yes, humans can get dog heartworms and it clogs up the heart in humans just like you see in the model at the veterinarian's. Hanna said that this is very hard on the heart because, according to her, the heart is fed from the inside and that is why the bypasses only help 50 percent of the time. To clean the heartworms out of the body, she suggests Sassafras tea or using Tea Tree oil, or Wormwood. The last two are very hard on the body so they are usually combined with other herbs for healing. She also has a vibrational remedy called *Heartworm* that does the trick.

* * *

The Simplicity of Herbal Health

Hanna Kroeger was against blood transfusions because she felt that blood is the carrier of life. It carries your family's DNA. So when you get a blood transfusion, you are taking on the problems of the donor's family history. Example, If I were to give blood to you, I would be giving you DNA that has weaknesses in the heart, pancreas and a few other areas that you really don't need. Hanna felt that one should ask oneself, "Is this truly needed?" You will be tied to that person for life because the blood is not your own, it carries hidden miasmas (Something handed down as in "to the seventh generation").

There is also a spiritual something transferred. A friend of ours received a heart transplant and went from the nicest person you would ever want to meet to a grumpy, demanding person. It is nice to think that you are helping to save a person who has abused their bodies for an entire lifetime but it would be in everyone's best interest to teach them to heal the body part in question.

Hanna suggested a few ways around the transfusion.

Use 1 tablespoon of Black Strap Molasses in 8 oz. of water, add lemon to taste and drink 4 oz. every half-hour. (4 oz. of anything will go into the blood stream fast, more than that doesn't.)

or

2 oz. of port wine with pumpernickel bread will also build the blood quickly.

* * *

Phyllis Heitkamp Master Herbalist

Herbs for the Brain

Let's discuss some herbs that assist the brain.

Gotu Kola, is a wonderful "Brain" herb. What do we mean by a "Brain" herb? We mean that it tends to go to the head of the body to find a way out of the body. Different herbs tend to do that. They have a specific area they feel would be great for exiting the body.

According to James Duke, "Gotu Kola is widely used in India to improve memory and extend longevity." I went into his Database and saw that he has identified 89 constituents for this herb. Both Dr. Duke and Dr. Werback stated that this herb has properties that are anti-parkinsonian and antielipeptic. Sounds like a great herb for the brain. It is also suggested that it has anti-Alzheimer's properties but just keeping cells healthy in the brain would do that. I have heard that "tags drugs" have been given to Alzheimer's patients and later when the brain has been examined, they find that new cells had been produced. We have been told in drug commercials that the brain does not re-grow. I understand the idea behind the commercials but the fact is that the brain cells are being replaced as fast as the cells are in other parts of the body, if one is giving nutrients to that area. When was the last time you fed your brain? We don't think about that and we need to.

Gotu Kola, with its 89 constituents, heads for the brain and will give nutrients that can be used to rebuild that area.

In addition, Longevity was mentioned. Some of the properties of this herb protect us from Cancers, Shingles, Virus, along with Tumors and in Duke's own words, "Antiaging".

Gotu Kola has been used for fatigue, memory, mental alertness and many things for the brain but it has properties that help with Tuberculosis, Vaginitis, Cervicitis, Leprosy and many more conditions.

Another wonderful thing that Gotu Kola can be used for is rebuilding collagen in skin. Duke mentions three of its 89 ingredients that do this. He suggests that it is great for burned skin and other wounds.

* * *

Rosemary is another "Brain" herb. "The Ancients were well acquainted with the shrub, which has a reputation for strengthening the memory," reports Mrs. Grieves in, <u>A Modern Herbal.</u>

My Mother had a stoke. The clot was on the left side of the brain. So her right side was paralyzed. She couldn't use her right leg. Her right arm was contorted and balled into her chest. On doing some research, I found that Mrs. Grieves talked about using Rosemary, allowing it to stand in wine for four days, then using it for circulation. She mentioned that this could be rubbed on hands and feet for Gout. She talked about Rosemary wine to be "taken in small quantities act as a quieting cordial to a weak heart.... By stimulating the brain and nervous system, it is a good remedy for headaches caused by feeble circulation. "

Knowing that it is also good for the Brain and can be used as a tonic, I put fresh Rosemary in my homemade Dandelion wine and allowed it to stand for a short while. (Whenever I say a short while, my students want to know how long that is. It is as long as a short while can be. One day to one week.) My sister, Betty, then gave it to Mother as a tonic. (Tonics being given in a tablespoonful once a day.) Within a week of this, Mother relaxed her arm and hand into her lap. I mentioned this to a fellow herbalist and she told me that she was working with a young lady in her late 20's who had a stroke a year earlier and wondered if I would make some of this tonic for her client. I did and I also made a disclaimer for the client to sign. I didn't hear anything about this for a while so I got the phone number of the client and called to see what results she was having. I reached the client's Mom. She told me that her daughter was sleeping and she didn't want to disturb her. I told her that I had made the tonic and wanted to know how it had worked. The Mom got excited and told me that since taking the tonic, her daughter's muscles had relaxed. Her daughter was now able to sleep more than three hours at a time. Before the tonic, her muscles were so contorted that she was always in pain.

Rosemary contains about 250 compounds, according to Dr. James Duke's Database. The USDA only recognizes a few of these such as Calcium, Iron, Magnesium, Phosphorus, Potassium, Zinc, Copper and Manganese.

Dr. Duke gets more in depth with things like Rosmarinic, Oleanolic Acid, and many more. He says that the active ones were very Antibacterial,

Antiherpetic. He mentions that Rosemary has AntiHIV along with Antiviral properties in a lot of the compounds contained in this herb. He also mentions that some of the compounds are calcium-antagonist but Rosemary also contains some Calcium. I found a lot of references to it being a cancer-preventive, anti-tumor and even Antiparkinsonian. This last one was referenced from <u>Healing with Foods</u>, by M. Werback, written in 1993.

The amount of constituents that were Fungicides were overwhelming. But it helped me to understand the connection with the anti-cancer properties. Hanna Kroeger talked a lot about the connection with fungus and cancer. The funny part is that as humans, inside we are a perfect breeding ground for fungus…moist and dark.

Perhaps the fact that Rosemary has so many things in it that attack fungus is important for all the fungus that seems to attack the brain. S.A.D. (Seasonal Affective Disorder) has been linked to a fungus called Coccideoidomycosis. Hanna created a vibrational to deal with this fungus it is called *Valliever*. It is believed that this fungus wraps around the pineal gland. Panic attacks have also been linked to fungi in the brain.

Cryptomycosis gets into the brain and makes the person feel "Foggy" (Alzheimer's?). Sometimes this fungus gets into the lungs, it likes the left lung more than the right for some reason. Sometimes it is even found in the spinal column. Hanna has a vibrational called *Cripto Funigus* to handle this problem. When there are brain changes like foggy thinking or panic attacks, there is usually a fungus-yeast relationship. Even Candida albicans can go systemic and create problems in the brain.

Because of its anticoagulant and antithyroid properties, found in a few of its over 200 properties, one might not want to make a meal of it but in general, Rosemary would be a great thing to grow and nibble on from time to time. It might take time to acquire a taste for it due to its tannins and other bitter properties but it has so much going for it that it is worth having some around.

* * *

Ginkgo is an herb that can be used for many things, the brain being one of them.

The Simplicity of Herbal Health

Unless you make your own tincture of Ginkgo, the commercial tincture of this herb is always standardized 50/1 for ginkoside. These herbs cross the blood/brain barrier both ways. Lots of drugs cross the blood/brain barrier into the brain but then tend to accumulate. When an herb is standardized, it will act like a drug, have side effect, and interact with medication.

In Europe, Ginkgo is the herb of choice for vascular disease, "...particularly Cerebral Circulatory disturbances and certain other peripheral arterial circulatory disorders," according to Dr. Varro E Tyler.

This plant is the oldest known plant on the planet. Most people believe that it is a dinosaur or at least from that age. There are some in China that are said to be hundreds of years old and still in very good health.

According to Dr. Tyler, one can not make a tea from the leaves of this tree and get the results that one wants because he feels that only the ginkoside is helpful in this plant. He does admit later in his article on Ginkgo that it might be the combination of a few of its other ingredients that are helpful. "The Therapeutic effects of GBE are attributed to a mixture of these constituents, not to a single chemical entity." (GBE= "A concentrated extract). Dr. Tyler also explains that the side effect of this GBE is nothing. He says that it could be gastrointestinal disturbances, headaches or an allergic skin reaction. Sounds more and more like the drug ads that I have seen than what I know about herbs.

I have seen things work that shouldn't work because they are not concentrated , but they do, so if you feel like making a tea out of your leaves, please do so.

* * *

An interesting thing that one finds in common with all of these herbs is that they contain organic aluminum. Aluminum is needed by the brain to rebuild. When the brain can't get it organically, it will go for the inorganic aluminum. This can come from your soda can...the acid in the can has absorbed the aluminum from the side of the can. Or it could come from the Aluminum foil that you cooked your food in or even just stored it in. But the Brain will steal it from somewhere. This is sort of like the little kid who eats mud because he is lacking something in his system.

Phyllis Heitkamp Master Herbalist

A good formula for a "brain tonic" might be:

2 Parts	Gotu Kola
1 Part	Ginkgo Leaf
1 Part	Peppermint leaf
½ Part	Rosemary or Sage

* * *

Dizziness can come from a lot of things. There can be a viroid (Smaller than a virus) in the brain. Or there could be a blood clot in the brain. Another thought is that it could be an inner ear problem.

My husband was working with me when all of a sudden he got very dizzy. I had him lie down and I checked his pulse. (Wanted to rule out a heart problem) Then I asked him to lift one leg at a time while I put pillows under each of them. I also had him hold the papers that I was using, first with one hand and then with the other. (Rule out a stroke) He told me that it felt really strange. He couldn't walk without tipping over. If he moved a lot, he got sick to his stomach. This did not surprise me, he gets motion sickness easily. He said that if he wasn't better by the next day, he wanted to go to the emergency room and find out what was happening to him.

The next day we went to the hospital. They ran all kinds of tests on him. By this time I have just about figured out what was happening when I over heard the man in charge calling my husband's doctor and telling him that all they found "was a high white count." I knew that we had a virus. He stayed there overnight for observation and the next day I picked him up. They gave me his papers and we talked about taking it easy for a while, then the nurse gave me a prescription for him to take. It was for Valium, a psychotic drug. Well, needless to say, I lost the prescription on the way home. After we got home, I started him on antiviral herbs. Soon he was back to normal.

Did you know that Chia Seeds are brain foods, and that Sesame Seeds help build strong minded people? Seeds are power foods. They contain everything to make the next generation of that plant.

* * *

The Simplicity of Herbal Health

Hanna was concerned about A.D.D. (Attention Deficit Disorder-Hyperactivity) She created the *New Light Kit* for this purpose. It contains Plumbum vibrational. (This is Latin for lead), and New Light viropathic liquid.

Hanna felt that Lead poisoning or MSG might cause Dyslexia.

Regarding coffee, Hanna felt that it was not good for a person to add milk but to use it with honey, as this combination would open the memory. Decaffeinated Coffee has too many chemicals in it to be drunk.

Hanna also talked about parasites that head for the brain. A few of them are Amoeba, Giardia, and Special-X. These are all Single-cell parasites, the last one is described as looking like a jelly fish that starts a small infestation in the spinal cord and then goes up to the brain. Hard to detect a parasite infection in the brain from a stool sample. Maybe we need better equipment?

There is a saying that people who have basil in their gardens will be fresh in the brain. Basil is brain food. I have a basil 'Minette' plant in my house and every time I walk by it, I have to take a deep breath of its scent. It is a wonderfully, fresh, clean, heady scent. So if we are not nibbling on our plants, maybe we should be smelling them?

Phyllis Heitkamp Master Herbalist

What is a Nervine?

I would like to talk a little about Nervines. Dr. John Christopher felt that:

"Nervine herbs act as nerve tonics. Their function is to feed, regulate, strengthen and rehabilitate the nerve cells. They act as either stimulants or sedatives, with the net result lessening the aberration, irritability or pain of the nervous system. These should not be confused with the inorganic narcotics or opiates used by orthodox physicians, which are eventually debilitating and damage life in the fiber and tissue." This is from his <u>School of Natural Healing</u> book.

*   *   *

In this area, I want to talk about my favorite Nervines.

The first is Valerian. Here is an old time remedy to relax the whole body. It has been used for more than one thousand years as a mild tranquilizer. With its ability to work on the cerebrospinal system, it is great for rebuilding the central nervous system for things like neuralgia pain, epileptic fits, hysteria, and much more.

It has also been employed to help with addictions, often being substituted for Valium to help mellow a person. This is why it is so good for anxiety and aggression. One bonus is that it is a great source of calcium and magnesium. Most of the nervines have Calcium and Magnesium. When checking Dr. Duke's Database, I found that he has 134 constituents listed for Valerian. Some of them are common things that you would recognize such as Chromium, Manganese, Niacine, Selenium, Linoleic – Acid, or Riboflavin, but the one that interested me was Aluminum. Organic aluminum is necessary for the brain. So this is one nervine that would target the brain.

It has the properties to slow the action of the heart while making it stronger. We have talked earlier about other herbs that have this property.

Valerian will also stimulate the peristalsis of the stomach and intestine, helping to clean up the body as a whole. As was said in the beginning of

The Simplicity of Herbal Health

this segment, Nervines not only sedate but stimulate as well. Once the nerves are rebuilt and working well, Nervines do whatever else is needed by the body.

* * *

Scullcap is another great nervine. I did my thesis on this herb. I had been trying to find out about different nervines because my Mother was taking 700 pills a month for Alzheimer's prescribed by a Psychologist and we were trying to find things that would help her relax that were natural.

The name Scullcap sounds dangerous. One thinks of Skull and Cross bones but in fact, the name comes from the Latin "Scutella' meaning a small dish. This referred to the shape of the flower.

It was one of the old-time remedies for Hydrophobia which gave it a common name of Mad Dogweed.

Scullcap or Skullcap, as it goes by both spellings, has been used for a long time to calm the nervous system without narcotic properties. It relieves spasms and tends to increase urine. It rebuilds nerve endings in the brain and has even been known to help with infertility according to Jack Ritchason in his book <u>The Little Herb Encyclopedia</u>..

It is slow working so in our "fast-acting" world, it might not be the herb of choice.

It helps with upper respiratory infections, blood poisons and it has been known to absorb toxins from the bowels. A lot of nerve "problems" are caused by toxic overload.

There are so many more things that it has been used for from helping a person stop smoking to helping them recover from a hangover.

No one should take the same nervine for a long time. With Mom, we found that doing some Skullcap for a while and then switching to Valerian was helpful. This way you are giving the body an assortment of constituents to choose from for the healing.

* * *

Wood Betony is wonderful. I really didn't think much about this herb until I was talking to another herbalist and she mentioned that she had a headache so she was going to leave and take some Wood Betony. I thought about that and decided to learn a little more about this plant, as that wouldn't have been my first choice to take for a headache.

Then I found out that it was used a lot for head and face pain, and that it is great with migraines.

I also found out that it is a great blood cleanser, as it will get obstructions out of the liver and spleen. Perhaps this is why the Greeks and Romans thought of this herb as a "cure-all".

* * *

Lobelia is most misaligned. Most herbalists know that it isn't dangerous but the FDA has put out warnings on this herb. They think that it can cause death. According to Dr. John Christopher, it can make you feel like you are dying if you misuse it but if used properly it is wonderful. Dr. Christopher talked about how he used it to help an asthmatic. He gave the person having the attack, 10 drops of tincture and then waited for 10 minutes. After the time was up, he gave the person another 10 drops of Lobelia tincture. Then waited another 10 minutes. In his lecture, he told us that in this ten minutes, he collected everything that would hold liquid. Then he gave the person 10 more drops, after which this person threw up the contents of his stomach, but that wasn't all, the person would continue to throw up, first the mucus that was in the bronchia and then from the lung area. He said that some of this mucus was green and had been clogging up the lungs for a long time. After this person had no more to throw up, he collapsed, probably thinking that he was dying. But according to Dr. Christopher, the former asthmatic never had another attack.

There is no record on file anywhere, which says that Lobelia has caused harm, but it is a powerful herb.

According to the good Doctor, you cannot take enough Lobelia to be poisoned. The body will not allow it. You will throw up. With this in mind, perhaps it would make a great herb to cleanse the body of poison recently taken?

The Simplicity of Herbal Health

Dr. Christopher calls lobelia a "thinking herb", because of this he uses it as a lead herb in many of his formulas.

One of his nervine tonics is called *Ear & Nerve Formula*. It contains 5 nervines and for this reason it is very useful at rebuilding nerve cells and the insulating sheaths around them. The Sheaths around the nerves are so important to keep the system from short-circuiting. Most of us don't take constituents that will help rebuild nerve cells and they are breaking down just like all the other cells in our body on a daily basis.

I used the nerve formula after breaking my wrist while rollerblading. When my arm came out of the cast, I wanted to regain the use of the thumb and it wouldn't work so I decided to exercise it. The muscles surrounding the thumb complained so I put a tissue paper on the area and dropped the above formula on it. I allowed it to soak into the skin and then removed the tissue paper. Now I could work the muscles without pain and they hadn't been anesthetized, just nourished.

Internally the nerve formula can be used for any nerve disorder, a twitching of the leg or face. It is the lobelia in this formula that takes the rest of the nervines to the specific area that needs rebuilding.

* * *

Now we have an herb that almost everyone has used at one time or another, and that is Hops.

Traditionally this herb has been used to provide a non-drug-induced sleep as it calms nerves. When Hops flowers are put into a pillow, they are used to prevent nightmares.

Hops is a great source of niacin. This is a B vitamin that most of us do not get enough of. Niacin is unequaled as a control for cholesterol. Niacin forces the LDL levels to drop in the body. It has also been acclaimed for tackling high triglycerides.

Hops is great at increasing the flow of urine and will tone the liver along with assisting a sluggish gallbladder. In this way it has been helpful for jaundice conditions.

It might be interesting to note that Hops can be used as a poultice on areas such as facial pain, sciatica and other rheumatic pains. It is also helpful with the pain of a toothache.

It is very relaxing as anyone who has had a nice cold beer can attest to.

* * *

One of Dr. Christopher's original formulas has been renamed *MindTrac*. I really hate that name but love the herbal combination. It contains: Valerian Root, Scullcap, Ginkgo Biloba, Oregon Grape, St. John's Wort, Mullein, Gotu Kola, Sarsaparilla, Dandelion, Lobelia, Jurassic Green (Composed of the powders of: Alfalfa, Barley and Kamut.) Some of these herbs we have already talked about, the others will be discussed in later chapters.

What is so great about this formula? It is an alternative to anti-depressant drugs and does no damage. We live in a world of stress. The world around us is filled with chemicals that have been known to severely damage the liver and other essential organs. "Rather than controlling the body through the manipulation of drugs, this formula uses nature's pure herbs to assist the body's emotional system to heal itself without the side effects of drugs."

In the past few years, I have found myself under a great deal of stress from one thing or another and the only way I have been able to deal with it, has been with *MindTrac*. As you can see by the herbs mentioned, it covers a lot of territory. It helps the nerves, the brain, the liver and other systems that we have not covered yet.

We all need help from time to time. But here is a "best friend" when your best friends are busy.

* * *

Shingles is a problem brought on by the nerves. It is a herpes/Chicken pox virus that has been dormant in the body until something triggers it to act on the nerve endings. Hanna Kroeger felt that the body needed more vitamins than it was getting or making. She felt that there was a lack of B-6 and B-12. She has a vibrational called *Shingazea* (interesting name for a

The Simplicity of Herbal Health

shingles remedy) to handle this problem. For the itching, Chickweed tea applied topically is very helpful.

Hanna talked about the fact that our bodies manufacture vitamins if we supply the building block to do so. When we take something containing beta-carotene, the right collarbone uses it to create Vitamin A.

Vitamin B-12 is manufactured in the left collarbone
Vitamin A is manufactured in the right collarbone
Vitamin E is manufactured in the long ribs
Vitamin D is manufactured in the sternum

Vitamin Deficiency
    Have problems in the a.m. (Parasites like vitamins)
Mineral Deficiency
    Have problems in the evening (Parasites don't like minerals)

* * *

There are some herbs that work to calm nerves that are not considered just Nervines and we will be talking about them in other areas of this book.

As a reminder, remember that there is only one dis-ease and that is constipation/congestion. We need to remember that getting the right things into the body helps to rebuild and keep us healthy.

Chapter III - Resources

Atkins, Robert C., MD, *Dr. Atkins' Vita-Nutrient Solution,* Fireside, NY., 1998, 407 pg.

Blake, Steven, *Global Herb-computer program,-Version 3.0,* California, 1995

Christopher, David, M.H. & Fawn, M.H., *A Healthier You – Audio Newsletter,* Christopher Publications, Springville, UT, 1999, 1-800-372-8255

Christopher, John R., Dr., School *of Natural Healing,* Christopher Publications,Springville, UT., 1976, 724 pg., www.snh.cc

Duke, James A. Ph.D., *Dr. Duke's Phytochemical and Ethnobotanical Database,* 2003

Grieve, M. Mrs., *A Modern Herbal,* Dover Publications, Inc., NY, 1971, 902 pg.

Reprinted with permission from *Back to Eden* by Jethro Kloss, Lotus Press, PO Box 325, Twin Lakes, WI. 53181, © 1999 All Rights Reserved.

Lycopene Research Updates, Lycopene.org - - Monthly Updates, 2003

Mowrey, Daniel B., Ph.D., *The Scientific Validation of Herbal Medicine ,* Keats Publishing, Inc., New Canaan, Connecticut, 1986, 3l1 pg.

Tyler, Varro E., Ph.D., *Herbs of Choice,* Pharmaceutical Products Press, 1994, 209 pg.

Chapter IV
Dandelion Wine

People have asked me about my Dandelion and Red Raspberry wines. After tasting them, they want to know how to make them so I start this chapter by teaching how to make Dandelion wine.

One of my rules is that you use what you have. Don't rush out and buy one hundred or two hundred dollars worth of equipment to experiment with making wine. Use what you have and have fun doing it.

As we enjoy making our products, the energy of the products will improve. People can tell the difference between something that has love injected into it and something that was just done to get it done. I believe there was a movie with this theme. When the cook cried into her food, the customers cried while eating it.

Another side to this is that if you go into a restaurant and there is a lot of noise (unfriendly sounds) coming from the kitchen, walk out and go somewhere else. The secret is to enjoy what you are doing or don't do it.

Step one is to take two grocery bags and fill them with Dandelion flowers. (note: where I live, the best time to pick them is in May.) There are dandelion flowers most of the Summer, but when they first come out and are very abundant is the best time to harvest. We find a place to pick that hasn't been sprayed with anything, including animal urine. We want our product to be clean.

The second step is to pull the petals off the flowers and put them into a large glass container. I use a large gallon olive/pickle jar that has been washed. When this is full of these beautiful yellow petals, hot water is poured over them and the jar is filled to the top with boiling hot distilled water. Why distilled water? Because distilled water is hungry water and will pull all of the wonderful constituents out of the dandelion petals. This is allowed to sit for 12 to 24 hours before straining the petals out of the infused water.

With the strained dandelion water back in the cleaned gallon container, the juice of one orange and two lemons is added along with one package of all-purpose yeast/wine yeast and 3 pounds of sugar for the yeast to live on. This then is covered with a cloth and a plate and allowed to process for 6 to 8 days or until it stops the fermentation process.

My secret is that I put this dandelion water into plastic gallon-water containers and put a balloon on the top instead of putting it back into the glass container. I have found that the large "punch-ball balloons" found in drug stores are perfect. They have an opening that is about an inch across and easily fits over the water container's top. These balloons also have a nipple on the top that is meant to tie a heavy-duty rubber band to so that a child can hold it and punch it. This nipple is very hard and is useful when the balloon is enlarging with gas coming from the wine making. When the balloon is partially inflated (about a foot in diameter), a small pinhole is placed in the nipple, allowing gas to be released slowly. When more gas escapes than the wine is making, the balloon starts to deflate, then it is time to bottle.

Have bottles ready and sterilize them by boiling them in hot water. Allow them to cool before bottling the wine. Also sterilize the caps or corks. Wine making stores have tablets that you can use to sterilize the bottles but boiling hot water has been used for this purpose for thousands of years and I feel it is still appropriate.

After the bottles are filled and corked or capped, it is time to label. Always label any of your homemade products. These labels can state what this product contains, the date it was made or anything else you would like to put on it. Or you can make it very simple by just stating that it is Dandelion Wine.

These wine bottles make great gifts. Have fun!

Harvesting and Storing

This chapter is about harvesting and storing but first let's talk about wildcrafting. This is when one harvests from the "wild" or country.

The first thing that is important is stewardship. Just as we would respect other people and their property, we need to give respect to plants. They are living things and very sentient beings. For some reason we have decided that they are the plant kingdom but, in fact, they are the plant kin-dom. We cannot live on this planet without them. We are meant to co-create with them on this planet. We have been told that we have dominion over them, when in fact, we are really supported by them. When we understand and respect plants, we influence their therapeutic value.

Communicating with Nature
We live in an intelligent environment and don't understand what this means. According to <u>The Third Wave</u>, written by Toffler; in which he states that many different peoples of the world believed, and some still do, that behind the immediate physical reality of things lie spirits, that even seemingly dead objects, rocks or earth, have a living force within them, *mana*. The Sioux Indians called it *wakan*. The Algonkians, *manitou*. The Iroquois, *orenda*. For such people the entire environment is alive.

According to Penny Kelly, " In a perfectly functioning world system no need goes unfilled, for the plants maintain a constant awareness of the animals and humans around them and respond intuitively to every possible condition. Their whole existence and purpose is to be there for you in every capacity, as food, as oxygen source, as companions, as artwork, as medicine, as spirit helpers, as protectors, to assist in your evolution, to open the connection to oneness, to smooth your births, to carry you out of the body when you choose to leave here, to facilitate communication with other forms, to remind you of your creative skills, to become your tools, and to be useful to you in a thousand other ways."

I have been reading <u>Native Plants Native Healing</u>, by Tis Mal Crow and he talks about listening to plants and talking to them. He mentioned that one should never complain about the taste of the plant when using it for medicine, he feels that then the product will not respond as needed.

Phyllis Heitkamp Master Herbalist

Plants and I have been best friends for a long time. As a small child, I would climb a tree when I felt sad or lonely and look out over the lake where we lived. I never felt that I was hanging on to the tree but that the tree was holding me. It was a comforting feeling. I also went up there when I knew that I was in trouble at home but Mom always knew where I was. We had a woods next door and to crawl under the bottom branches of a pine tree was a sacred place. It still is.

When I was reading Machaelle Small Wright's biography, <u>Behaving As If The God In All Life Matters</u>, I was hoping for more and then I got to the part where she started to hear the plants talking to her. She says that she was talking to the "Plant Deva" and for more information on that, you might read the book. When she talked to the plants and they responded to her and she, to them, I got all excited. So this is when I started to communicate with them.

Many people have communicated with plants and have received a response back.

Michael J. Roads, author of <u>Talking with Nature</u> talked about the questions that he had for nature. Some of our human guilt gets reflected in what we think these plants have to say to us. Michael talked about how he got corrected by nature regarding what we think. As an example, he talked about cutting down a Christmas tree for his daughter and it "reopened old wounds in my mind." But Nature put him at ease telling him to *"Relax, my friend. Do not be drawn into old thought patterns. Doubt is an established pattern of confusion which will deny your experience. Relax. I am not separate in consciousness from each separated physical tree you wish to take. Each tree can be likened to an aspect of "ones" consciousness. Within this is your challenge."*

My first introduction with this way of thinking came from a book called <u>The Magic of Findhorn</u> by Peter Cady about his creation in Scotland. He and two others worked with nature and were able to grow huge vegetables in sand using the instructions given by Nature.

My experience started with plant experiments. I tried different kinds of grafting after reading about John Muir, the naturalist. I read how some plants reacted on a polygraph when the plants next to them were set on fire. I knew that some day I would connect to that part of my world. There had to be more than what we saw every day.

The Simplicity of Herbal Health

One fall day, I was lying on the grass, watching the clouds tease the top of my double oak tree. The squirrels were running around collecting nuts. All the neighbors were raking leaves into piles. My husband was washing the storm windows. All of this activity made me feel very lazy so I said to the Oak tree of Oakwell, "I bet you know the secret of life." And I heard, " The secret of life is to make a place of peace and comfort for those around you." Time out... I just heard from a tree. And yes, isn't that what every tree does? (Penny Kelly just said the same thing.)

In <u>Perelandra - Garden Workbook</u>, also by Machaelle Small Wright, one can learn how to co-create with plants. How to communicate with them. After reading her book, I had a "feeling" that I needed to enlarge the small garden around our two apple trees. So I dug up more lawn around the garden that I now call the Apple Garden. (This garden was first created so my husband wouldn't have to mow close to these trees) It was early spring and the temperature was in the 40's but I was dressed for it and warm as I pulled the angleworms out of the sod and shook the dirt out. I threw these clumps, along with the stones that I found, onto the lawn. When I had it just the right size, I mixed in some peat moss and some composted manure. It was like mixing biscuit dough. I was so proud of this little garden, so I backed up to look at all of it and in doing so, I saw heat waves rising from the whole area. It looked like it was about to lift off and float into space. I ran into the garage and brought back a cement slab. Then I went around the little garden, picking up all the walnut-sized rocks, putting them on the slab. Standing back once more, the heat waves were gone. The area had been grounded. It felt good.

I wrote to Machaelle Small Wright telling her what happened and she wrote back telling me that most people just read this stuff and never do anything about it. She was happy that I responded to the "feelings" that the plants were sending me.

Many years later, our Oak tree became infested with Gypsy Moths. I did a lot of research and called on people from the State Parks Service to help me but because we do not allow sprays on our property, they couldn't help me. My first line of defense was to put molasses in a 4 inch band around the trunk of the oak tree.(Our tree took two jars of the molasses.) This slowed the caterpillars down, then we picked them off.

The next thing that I did was to import predators. I found a very small wasp (Trichogramma) that eats these egg masses and lays their eggs inside of the caterpillars. So I imported a lot of them. The tiny wasps came by the 5,000 in a small container that one would put mustard. They looked like pepper when they arrived and I was told to put them by plants that have multiple tiny flower heads. The front yard Yarrow was just right.

The DNR (Department of Natural Resources) was very upset because I had imported something not found here. I got a letter dated October of 1999 and they said in effect that these would not work because the "Gypsy moth eggs are covered with a felt of hairs that prevent Trichogramma from successfully parasitizing them." This edict has been changed as my husband just read (four years later) in the paper that one should not remove the egg masses, as insects will destroy them. My feeling was that Gypsy Moths have just started to live in our state and are on their way west, they are not going to be stopped here. The DNR has since instituted a mass aerial spraying of some chemical.

I just finished <u>Silent Spring</u> by Rachel Carson and the spraying didn't stop the Elm problem or the Gypsy Moths on the East Coast in the '50s, but did "control" duck and bird populations along with many other small animals in the area of the spraying. It seems that aerial spraying has never really done the job but it is continued to this day.

In the meantime, I found a soy spray that was developed in a southern state. They said that it would seal the egg masses but would not hurt the trees. I talked to my arborist and he said that if I gave him the information, he could probably get a deal on it. We needed his bucket truck to put it on the egg masses that were 30 to 50 feet off the ground so he ordered it and put it on our tree. I am sure that he used it for his other customers who were having this same problem.

My husband wanted to spray the following year and I was torn between saving this huge oak tree and the spraying. I called Perelandra (the Nature Research Center founded by Machaelle Wright) and told them about our "War" with the Gypsy Moths. The first thing that they told me was to "STOP WARRING." I was told to find out from the moths what they would need to stay healthy and not over-run the tree and what the tree would need to stay healthy and handle this invasion.

The Simplicity of Herbal Health

We are a few years into this now and there are only a few moths on the tree this year. I don't know the reason, as there could be many. The county is "warring" with this species. The State is trying to hold the line of the westward movement of this insect. Has nature ever listened to politicians?

Listening to plants can be fun and informative. I found at first that I could do it through automatic writing. I would write a question and wait for the answer. Little by little, one word at a time would come into my head. I would write it down and wait for the next word. Being a problem solver, I always tried to guess what the next word would be. " You...Should..." and I would think something like....clean up the garden but instead the next word would be "Move" (now I have it....move the crowded geraniums) but the next word would be "Rocks". OK, now I know what they want. They want the rocks to be moved to another area. "..In to.." into what? "..A fairy.." A fairy? "..Circle." Well, of course, I should place the rocks into a fairy circle. When I have asked if this or that would be better, most of the time, they have made me decide for myself. They do like to play games with me by popping plants in the most unusual places and a long way from where they were the year before.

When they have communicated in this manner, at first I thought I was talking to myself but I was getting information about things of which I had no knowledge. One of the most important and prevalent things that they would tell me was "We are one." Always the "We are one" and I have tried to incorporate this in my way of thinking. It is not you and I, it is we. Plants and animals (people included in this) are the beings on this planet. We are all one.

I also found that they like our energy. By putting my hands parallel to each other and move them back and forth, I created energy between them. Try this: hold your hands together. Now pull them apart about one half inch. Close your eyes and move your hands in different directions still keeping the small distance between them. Do you feel the energy? I would throw this energy in the direction of any plant that has been newly planted or transplanted. They have told me that they can use this energy in the same manner that they can use the sun's energy.

When my husband is going to trim something, I have asked him to inform the tree/bush what is going to happen, then he is to come in and get something to drink. That will give the plant time to assimilate the information. If the plant is to be cut down, a three-day notice is required for the spirit of that tree to leave. I know that most of you will find this strange but we need to treat these beings as our brothers, remembering that without them, we cannot breath. It is time that we start to respect all living things. We have not been doing that for a very long time. But then most people that I know even take their close family relationships lightly.

One of the most interesting things about plants is their energy force. The best time to see the energy of a tree or plant is late on a warm summer's night. How did Shakespeare put it? "A mid-summer night's...." If you will relax and look around you, you will see different colored lights dancing. They come in all colors and shapes. According to M. Wright, these are the Deva's of the plants and animals. (Deva, being a Sanskrit word for, being of light.) I like to think of them as the plant's angels.

While doing my automatic writing, I write by the light of one candle, at night after the world is tucked in. One night my cats were running this way and that way. I asked what my cats were chasing and was told that they were chasing the beings that I was talking to. So I asked what they looked like to my cats and was told that they saw little sparks of light, much like lightening bugs, I assumed.

Recently, we had been having long periods of drought in our area. Not to the point of losing plants but where a lot of things like Wild Ginger and my mints are drooping. In Penny Kelly's book, Robes...she said, " Trees and vegetation are other critical elements in moderating and controlling electromagnetic fields, and therefore the wind. Trees are themselves producers of magnetic fields, and their fields interact with the magnetically charged pockets of air and land in two main ways.

One is that they keep air moving through sheer intelligence. Trees are intelligent beings capable of shifting the electromagnetic signature of the E-M fields they produce. Thus, they are capable of attracting air pockets containing moisture when they are dry and want something to drink."

After reading this, I told my large trees, Oak, Maple, and Locust, that they were not doing their job. They are supposed to bring in rain for the other beings around them. I gave them quite a tongue-lashing and to my surprise, within 24 hours, we got water. First, it was a sprinkle, followed by an all day easy rain. Boy, did I feel foolish. Then I had to go out and apologize to them. It didn't make any difference what the weatherman had

The Simplicity of Herbal Health

to say about the situation, as they had been promising rain for a week but the trees really did it.

*　*　*

Harvesting

When headed out to harvest, it is wise to carry a couple of small books for identification. One such book is <u>Peterson's Field Guide to Eastern/ Central Medicinal Plants</u> by Foster and Duke. The drawings in this book are very precise and helpful. Sometimes, in photos, the leaves are hard to see clearly, so I prefer drawings.

The other book that I find helpful is called <u>Herbs</u>, by Lesley Bremness. This one has pictures and drawings of plant parts to help identify easier.

Another book that is helpful is <u>National Audubon Society Field Guide To North American Wildflowers – Eastern Region,</u> Knopf, publisher. This book also has some wonderful photos but the written description is so very detailed that it is easy to use for identification. I have not found it as helpful as the first books mentioned because this book puts plants in families and unless you are aware of the family that it belongs in, it is hard to locate.

I try harvesting only one kind of plant at a time when I go out. That way I know what it is. If on the way to something, I find a stand of something else that I need, I note where it is and keep that in mind for the next trip. This way, I can process these herbs while they are fresh. If I had a lot of different ones to process, I might not be giving my medicine the attention that it deserves.

Herbal medicine is sacred. A life has been given to create it. Up until reading this, most people feel that we are just involved with some plants, "so what?" But that gets us back to our original line of thought that plants are living, sentient beings. We all agree that it is wrong to kill but we do it all the time. We have to do it to survive. This is why I am not a vegetarian. Vegetarians don't want to eat living creatures but have no such compulsion to killing wheat or taking the future generations of the oat plant. We need to be aware that food comes from the death of another species. This is the reason to give thanks for our food, not just that it is abundant and supplied to us but that it was obtained from the sacrifice of another species.

When Native Americans harvested plants, they left a bit of tobacco as a "Thank you" to Nature. I carry dried Comfrey leaves and use them in this manner. (Make sure that your "gift" is not Comfrey root as even small pieces of this root tends to grow wherever it finds itself.)

The rules to wildcrafting are to keep your picking place a secret and never harvest unless there are more than 10 plants. And if there are only 10, you are allowed one. This is the only way to show respect and make sure that they will be here year after year. There are always exception to every rule and one of these is that if you have only 3 plants, you are allowed one or two leaves from each plant. The leaves are the plant's food manufacturing plant for growth and rebuilding so leave as many as you can. Some plants have very big leaves and one large leaf might be sufficient for what is being made.

The breaking of this rule is how a lot of our plants became endangered. One such plant family that I can think of is the orchid family. For the most part, in the orchid family, the flower is an extension of the leaf stem and when a person picks the flower of Lady Slipper or Trillium, they are taking the leaves with them. Then there are no leaves left to rebuild the bulb and the whole plant dies.

If larger quantities of a certain plant are needed, it is best to order from organic growers or grow your own. Many of us grow the amount that we need or know people who have what is needed growing on their properties in large quantities.

This is part of the changes that are taking place on this planet. We are learning to be cooperative, to help one another. We have been taught to be competitive where we should have been taught to be cooperative. Survival depends on helping each other, not on corporate ladder climbing.

There is a proper time to harvest and the best time is in the morning hours, after the morning dew has dried and before the sun has pulled the energy from the plant's roots to the growing tips.

Because we don't want to process more water than is necessary, we don't harvest on rainy days. Another reason for this is because some of the water-soluble properties of these plants will have been washed away and it will take time for the plants to replace these constituents.

The Simplicity of Herbal Health

There is even a season for harvesting certain things. In the springtime, it is time to harvest buds and new leaves of plants. Late spring, we harvest just opened flowers and leaves along with some bark. When it is summer, we harvest plants, leaves and bark. Then in the fall, we harvest seeds and roots.

Again, these rules are rules of thumb so if you need a root in the spring or bark in winter it is there for you, but maybe not as potent as it would be in its season.

Rules are wonderful in so far as they constitute order but they have to make sense. Again we have been trained to OBEY the rules. Plants are very forgiving and if you need something that is important to you, they don't know the rules.

When harvesting, check to see what part of the plant would do what you intend this medicine to do. One of the best set of books for this are <u>A Modern Herbal - Volumes 1 & 2</u> by Mrs. Grieves. Every herbal library should include her books. She not only tells the history of the plant but what part is used for what and how to make it.

When harvesting bark it is advisable to use a branch that has been or needs to be severed from the tree of the species that is needed. If that isn't possible, the next best thing is to take bark off the trunk of the tree. Because it is the inner bark of the tree that has the medicinal properties and it is this same inner bark that is the "blood" system of the tree, it needs to be taken off in a careful manner. Never take bark off in a circular manner or around the trunk, as this will cut the "blood" supply to the upper tree.

Two long vertical cuts about 4 inches or less away from each other are made in the trunk or large branch. Cut through the outer bark and inner bark until you are cutting into the wood itself. Then connecting cuts can be made at the top of these and again at the bottom, making a long strip of bark for your medicine.

I have found that when I need bark, my "tree" man will bring a log of the type of tree that I need and I can harvest all of the bark on it without hurting a living tree. When I need Oak bark, I call and tell him to keep me in mind when he is working on an Oak tree. Sometimes I find a branch that has been "downed" during a storm. These can be stripped of the inner bark. This happened with a willow in my neighborhood.

By cutting narrow, long strips, I can peel the inner bark from the outer bark quite easily. Larger cuts are harder to handle. Also by having the inner bark strips small, it is easier to dry them.

* * *

Storing

Let's talk about processing the products that we have harvested. One of the ways to keep herbs available for use when they are needed is to dry them.

There are many ways to dry herbs. Most of us think about hanging them upside down and letting these air-dry. I have found that this just won't work in my area. I would end up with plant matter that would be loaded with spider webs or just any kind of bug. This would not work for making medicine for my family and myself. I don't want to process bugs too.

Using a large paper grocery bag, I put my plant matter in it. Then I label the bag and bending the top over, I either paper clip or staple the top. This way nothing is getting in. Every day I shake this bag up and set it down on a different side. The moisture of the plant matter dampens the bag and is released. When the plants in the bag are dry and the bag no longer gets damp, I check the contents and if they are completely dry, they are then placed in a glass container. Glass is the best material as it doesn't add or subtract anything from my dried herbs. If, on the other hand, they are placed in the glass before they are completely dry, they will mold and not be usable.

Another drying method is the oven. By laying the leaves on a paper-towel-lined cookie sheet and turning the oven to warm (just before heat settings on the dial), then putting a wooden spoon in the door so that it can not shut all the way, (allowing the moisture to escape) one can dry a large batch of leaves in part of a day. It is helpful to move the leaves a few times while they are drying.

There are herb dryers or food dryers that can be used to speed up the process. In them you can dry more than one herb at a time. They also have herb-drying settings on them.

* * *

Making A Tincture

Drying isn't the only way to store plant matter for a long time. **Tinctures** are able to preserve the properties of herbs for up to 40 years if they have been sealed and not opened, according to Dr. John Christopher.

To make a **tincture** we need two things, a solvent and something to pull the properties from. In the herbal lexicon, the menstrum is the solvent and the marc is the herbal material being used.

Using this idea one could call a tea, a **tincture** where the marc is the tea bag and the menstrum is water.

Another example could be garlic vinegar. Here we put garlic cloves (marc) in vinegar (menstrum). There are many ways to make **tinctures**. Mine will be a simplified version.

* * *

The herb or marc we will use today will be St. Johns Wort. So let's learn a little about it.

As of the writing of this chapter, the St. Johns Wort in my yard is budded and ready to open those tiny, five-petaled yellow flowers. I mention that because the plant is green with yellow flowers, but after it is made into a tincture and the active ingredients are extracted, the tincture is a beautiful clear ruby-red color. One of the ways to identify this plant is through this coloration. By crushing the leaves, I have had the skin on my fingers become quite red.

St. Johns Wort has gotten a bad reputation from over use in recent times. Most people associate it with its sedative abilities. With this ability, it can be used for pain.

In the past few years it has been used extensively for depression only to find that most people don't understand how to use it properly. We have been brought up to believe that if a little is good then a lot is better. In the case of St. Johns Wort, a little is best. Most herbs can be thought of this way and by taking just a little we are helping our bodies a lot.

It has the ability to increase the blood flow to areas in need, thereby activating areas that have not been working. When we supply areas with nutrients that are lacking, everything works better.

One of the wonderful qualities of this herb is its ability to heal wounds that are dirty or have been around so long that they have putrefied the skin. St. Johns Wort has the ability to clean out the dirt and reduce the inflammation while not destroying any healthy skin.

In <u>The little Herb Encyclopedia</u> by Jack Ritchason N.D., it is listed as being, Anti-bacterial, Anti-depressant, Anti-fungal, Anti-inflammatory, Anti-spasmodic, Anti-tumor, Anti-viral, Astringent, Diuretic, Expectorant, Nervine, Sedative, and Vulnerary *(The dictionary says that this word means, "Used in the healing or treating of wounds".)* Most of us only think of St. Johns Wort as an anti-depressant.

According to Alma Hutchens in <u>Indian Herbalogy of North America</u> , "An old custom of our Indians was to dry Hypericum (St. John's Wort) and use it as a meal, as they did acorns. They were also known to eat the fresh leaves for their soothing effect. In many cases of bronchitis, it has been known to eliminate all signs of the condition. St. John's wort can be administered to all, whatever age or sex and was at one time found in almost every country household. For treatment of dysentery, diarrhea, bleeding of the lungs, worms, jaundice, suppressed urine and/or pus in the urine, hysteria and nervous irritation." She just said that it could be used by everyone and yet at the present time people are having problems with this wonderful herb.

Lets do the "why" right here before we continue to talk about this or other herbs.

Scientists found that it was the compound Hypericin that was doing all of these good things. So since 1042, they have isolated it from St. Johns Wort and created a new medicine. It is called St. Johns Wort – Standardized. Most of the time they standardize the product to 50% on the constituent that they feel you need. Now we have a drug because the constituents of this plant are no longer in balance. When they standardize an herb, they add what they feel is needed of this herb to a capsule or tincture to have a certain percentage of the active ingredient.

The Simplicity of Herbal Health

When I checked Dr. James Duke's Database on this herb, I found that there are 64 compounds in this plant. The ingredient that they standardize to is Hypericin, only one of the 64 constituents. When something is this out of balance, it is a drug and will cause side effects.

This is the "why" of making your own medicine, of making your own St. John's Wort tincture. The part used is the flowering tops. It will not be standardized and will therefore be healthier for the things that you want to use it on. We don't need side effects.

It would be wise to mention that it is possible to take St. Johns Wort and have a sensitivity to sunlight but when making it in its wholesome state, this sensitivity will be lessened by the interactions of the other constituents in this plant. Varro Tyler, In his book, <u>Herbs of Choice</u>, mentions that animals eating St. Johns Wort have been known to have skin problems when exposed to sunlight, but he also says that not a single case has been reported involving humans. I have heard that the people who harvest it for a living, do become sensitive to sunlight by the absorption of the plant properties through their skin. But we also read that Native Americans used it for food.

Making the tincture

One of the first rules in herbal medicine is that it should be safe to use, even if it is accidentally used wrong. We are not trained in that manner and therefore we fear that we might make a mistake. Herbal health should be fear-free. With drugs, one can have a lot of problems if they are used incorrectly.

I don't teach about dangerous plants, so everything that I talk about is safe. It is nice to know which ones are dangerous but in this book, we are talking about healing.

Using fresh St. Johns Wort (marc), we will fill our glass container one-third full of this plant material. (I like using 8 to 10 oz juice bottles.) Next we fill up the bottle with the 100 proof Vodka (menstrum) until the bottle has about 1 inch to ½ inch left at the top and then cover the bottle. Label it. Now it is ready to be started. For the next 14 days, it needs to be shaken up from time to time. This makes sure that the marc doesn't settle to the bottom and stay there the whole 14 days and that the menstrum is mixed nicely with the marc so as to get to all the surfaces of the plant matter. We want to pull out as much of the plant's constituents as is possible. Some of my students shake their preparation twice a day and others once a day. When using other materials such as dried and/or powdered material, it is very necessary to shake this up a lot as the dried matter tends to settle more than the fresh does.

Our menstrum is always a grain alcohol. I use 100 proof vodka. Vodka was originally made from wheat mash but now it is also made from the mash of rye, corn and in Russia it is made from potatoes. All of which are edible. Why 100 proof? Because 100 proof is 50% water and 50% alcohol. The regular vodka that is used for mixing drinks is 80 proof. This just means that it is 40% water and 40% alcohol and 20% of "God only knows what" (it isn't labeled), we don't want "God only knows what" in our medicine.

This is why I use only 100 proof vodka or Everclear (another all-grain alcohol). With our menstrum, one doesn't have to decide if it can be taken internally or externally only. I always wondered why people would call me to see if they can use the tincture that they made in class for a toenail fungus, internally too.

Having just read <u>Native Plants Native Healing- Traditional Muskagee Way</u> by Tis Mal Crow, I have to mention how he does some of these things. In this wonderful book he uses isopropyl alcohol for some of the tinctures, the ones that will be used externally. Isopropyl is not good to be put into the body.

When using St. Johns Wort, as the healing properties are drawn out, the alcohol will turn a beautiful "port wine" red.

After the 2 weeks are over, it is time to finish the process of making an herbal tincture. Using a strainer lined with cloth, (I use cotton squares) the contents of the bottle is dumped in the strainer, and by pulling the corners of the cloth up, squeezing all of the liquid out, every drop is being used. Then the liquid or alcohol containing all of the usable constituents of whatever marc we have used will be put into dropper bottles; labeled and ready for use. These labels might contain the contents, where they were obtained and the date made, for future reference.

These bottles can be dipped in melted wax to seal them for storage. Dr. Christopher has kept some of his preparation for up to 40 years this way.

The Simplicity of Herbal Health

The rule of thumb for taking tinctures is 10 to 12 drops in water, three times a day or as needed.

According to Tis Mal Crow, all tinctures should be cut as he feels that they aggravate problems when used full strength. On the other hand, Dr. Richard Schultz of the Los Angeles area, who is a practicing herbalist and also a student of Dr. John Christopher's, feels that "herbalists are wimps", his words. He feels that when one is around sick people, that is the time to take Echinacea tincture in the manner that is stated on the bottle – 5 to 10 drops, three times a day. He feels that when you think you are getting sick, you take 10 to 20 drops of Echinacea tincture. When you are sick, you take a two ounce bottle, divide it in half and down (drink) half of it right away and take the rest of the bottle in drops over the rest of the day. He feels that this process will "jump-start" the immune system. So I will leave it up to you to decide what you should do. I will continue to use them at full strength in the 10 to 15 drops as needed.

Dr. Christopher told us that herbs could be used every hour when there is an emergency. Remember that Herbs are foods in their wholesome state. They can be prepared any way except altered by standardizing, which makes them "part-some", not wholesome.

Black Walnut

I have another herb that is so helpful that I would like to take some space here to tell you how to prepare it and that is Black Walnut Tincture.

This is another one of my "Big Guns" because it is antibiotic, anti-fungal, anti-parasitic, and anti-viral. A first aid kit in a bottle. Having a small tincture with me all the time is helpful. When I am traveling and I am not sure of the water source, a dropper full of Black Walnut Tincture in the water, will give me a good feeling because I have just gotten rid of bacteria and parasites in that water.

I didn't know that it handled virus until my sister, Betty came to live in my area. At that time she was covered with warts. She started applying the Black Walnut Tincture to each of the warts topically and taking it internally. After about a month of doing that, we were at lunch and a wart fell off her body from near her eyebrow and landed next to her plate. I told her how "gross" that was so she explained to me that when she was showering that morning, many fell off her torso.

To create your own Black Walnut tincture, one must pull (Yes, I said pull) immature fruit off a Black Walnut tree. This is done when the fruit reaches full size. The more immature, the better. Next, one needs to slice through the fruit, cutting it in half. Now the fruit is cut into quarters or smaller and put into a glass jar, filling the jar one-third of the way full. Cover all of this up to within an inch of the top with vodka, cap the jar, and labeling it at this time. (It is necessary to always label.)

If the fruit is not immature, it will not be possible to cut it up in the manner suggested above. In that case, the flesh is cut away from the nut and the flesh is put into the jar, much like cutting the flesh off an avocado, processing this as suggested earlier for the whole fruit.

Within a short time, the clear vodka will get very dark as the organic iodine is being pulled out of this product. This can be used just like the old Mercurochrome that your Mom used to put on your sores to kill bacteria and start the healing, and it stings just like the old stuff did too.

Another use for Black Walnut Tincture is to increase organic Iodine in the body. People who live on coastal areas of our country tend to eat more seafood and thereby get iodine in their system but those of us who live in the middle of the country, will find there are few foods that we eat containing iodine. Iodine is very necessary to the health of the thyroid and its functions.

Dr. Christopher told us that Black Walnut Tincture was high in Potassium and suggested that if we want to give more Potassium to our families, a few droppers full put into soups and stews would do the trick.

When we put the **tincture** into hot water, the alcohol will dissipate, leaving only the herbal constituents.

Herb Walk

After making a tincture, I usually take the class on an herbal walk. If the weather is nice we do it outside. If it isn't nice, or it is in the middle of the winter, we do the "Walk" with my pressed plants.

So let's "walk" through my garden of herbs and visit with a few of my friends.

Alfalfa

This plant is loaded with nutrients for our bodies. According to Alma Hutchens, this plant is not a native of North America but at present it is found everywhere on this continent. She mentions that it has the ability to spread its roots as far as 125 feet below the surface of the earth to obtain all these nutrients. When a plant can stretch itself that far, it has a right to be called "Father of all foods."

When I was much younger, my Aunt Eunice was encouraging everyone in the family to take Alfalfa tables for just about everything. I guess she knew that it contained Calcium, Magnesium, Phosphorus and Potassium, plus all the vitamins including Vitamin K and P.

It has a way of balancing the body to assist it in maintaining or regaining health.

Another case of supplying the body with the nutrients and it will rebuild.

* * *

Basil

Hanna talked about the fact that Basil was wonderful for the brain, for helping us stay on top of things, mentally

Varro Tyler tells us that the leaves of basil can be "Simply rubbed against the teeth to inhibit plaque formation and to treat periodontal disease."

Many countries felt that Basil was a sacred herb. When I look at what it is capable of doing, I can understand their feelings.

We know that it has the ability to eliminate parasites in our bodies. By macerating it, one can put it on an insect bite to draw out the poison and it has antibacterial properties

Because it is also antispasmodic, it has been used for whooping cough, stomach cramps, spasms, croup, indigestion, nervous conditions and to assist the liver.

For women, it has been used for suppressed menstruation and cramps.

And we just thought Basil was just good in the kitchen. I am always amazed at all the things these little plants are capable of doing. (And they even taste good.) I can't imagine going to the drug store for anything. No, not even for aspirin, as basil is good for headache too. (Although my all time favorite for a headache is Wood Betony)

* * *

Calendula

Calendula is a member of the marigold family so it has similar characteristics. The difference is that the flower head isn't like the hybrids that one sees in the seed catalogues. This flower head is more sunflower in shape.

One of the interesting things about Calendula is that it has been used for healing so long that when doctors started using drugs and harsh chemicals, they were able to make them work by relying on old favorites such as this one to handle the gross side-effects that were happening.

Nicholas Culpepper found that mixing the leaves with vinegar would give instant relief on "Hot Swellings". This same juice was found to be good at cleaning toxins out of the liver.

Most of the time we use the petals of this plant because they create a soothing sensation to the body both inside and out. Herbal skin creams

The Simplicity of Herbal Health

usually have Calendula in them for this very reason. One could make an infusion (Tea) with these petals and use it as a soothing eyewash.

These same petals have been used to color foods and are used to stimulate the immune system as well as Echinacea does. Other properties of these yellow petals are those of being antiseptic and antifungal. It goes beyond that in alleviates pain. According to Jack Ritchason, "Old herbal doctors believed that constant applications of Calendula would help or even prevent gangrene or tetanus."

Hanna recommends a Calendula combination for tumors or ulcers.

Most commonly the petals are crushed and applied to skin that has been bruised or burned. It can even made into an ointment for varicose veins.

Jack Ritchason states that it would be good for Abrasions, Acne, Athletes foot, Bee stings, Bleeding, Blood purifier, Bug bites, Burns, Cancer and even Chickenpox.

Hanna suggests making an herbal tea from Calendula and combining it with olive leaves and yarrow whenever you have a virus infection like hepatitis.

* * *

Evening Primrose

This weed grows anywhere it wants to in my yard. I nibble on the flowers and enjoy the benefits that it wants to give me. Except for the flowers, I don't think that the plant itself is pretty but let me tell you what it can do.

This plant is a native to North America and is found in ditches, fields and wasteland everywhere. It has been called a "cure-all" by many people. It propagates by seeds and because of its scruffy look, with its lovely yellow flowers, it would be best suited for a place in the back of ones herb garden. It has been known to grow as tall as 5 to 7 feet but I have always seen the 3 to 4 foot plants.

Native American's use the plant for everything from bruises to hemorrhoids.

According to Steven Foster, "The Shakers, who established the first commercial herb business in the United States, listed Evening Primrose roots in many of their catalogs as a vulnerary, demulcent, mucilage, and stomachie."

Modern use of the plant has focused on the seed oil, and more specifically its GLA (gamma-linolenic acid) content."

Almost everyone has heard of Primrose Oil and most know of its high content of essential fatty-acids. According to my <u>Merck Manuel</u>, "Many nutrients can be synthesized in the body. Those that can't be synthesized in the body - called essential nutrients – must be consumed in the diet. They include amino acids (in protein), certain fatty acids (in fats and oils), minerals and vitamins."

* * *

Garlic - Onion

One of my favorite herbal families is the Garlic/onion family. Garlic has been used, loved, or hated through the centuries. Mrs. Grieves tells of a superstition that says if a runner is chewing some garlic while in a race, his competitors will not be able to get ahead of him. She also mentions that it was used a lot in 1916 as an antiseptic for the war effort. They used it by juicing it and using the juice on wounds.

Garlic was also the principle ingredient in the "Four Thieves' Vinegar that was used in 1722 in France during the plagues. Dr. Christopher has a product that is called *Immune Support Formula* (formerly called Anti-Plague) that contains: fresh garlic juice, wormwood, lobelia, marshmallow, white oak bark, black walnut bark, mullein, aloe vera, uva ursi, skullcap and raw honey. My daughter, Kathy and my sister, Donna tell me that it is "God-awful". But it works and I have used it myself with much success, when everyone else is recycling the flu.

Let's talk about how garlic works. It softens the walls of cells. Isn't that simple? We have all heard of some people who can tell about the weather by the way their body feels. They will say something like, my knee tells

The Simplicity of Herbal Health

me that we are getting a storm soon. What is happening is that as the air pressure is dropping (pending storm), and the pressure inside the cells stay the same. So like a balloon, the cells in that area are expanding due to the lowering pressure outside of the cells and they are squeeze the local nerves. (Pain) When the cell walls are hard, nothing can get in and nothing can get out. When Garlic softens the cell walls, the cells can absorb nutrition and release waste matter and balance the pressure.

That is all there is to healing the body. Get nutrition in and toxins out and we are back to Dr. Christopher's original theory...there is only one disease...Constipation or congestion and it can be anywhere.

I checked with Duke's database and found that there are over 200 different things in Garlic that allows it to do what it does. A lot of them had "Immunostimulator" properties and there quite of few things that were Antibacterial or Antibiotic. The surprise was how many of its properties were either antioxidant or antitumor or both.

To make garlic oil, one would crush garlic cloves and put them into a jar, filling the jar with olive oil. Close tightly and shake a few times each day for 3 days. This can then be dropped into the ear for its antibacterial and antifungal properties.

I heard a tape by Dr. Richard Schultz where he suggested that if one had a vaginal yeast infection, a large clove of Garlic should be inserted before bedtime. He suggested an herbal douche in the morning and repeating this for a few days. After the first night, one would score the clove before inserting it to allow more of the juice to work during the night. Hanna suggests this same thing for Hemorrhoids.

Hanna tells us in her <u>Heal Your Life With Home Remedies and Herbs</u>, that, "Garlic (is a) natural antibiotic; (it) has M-rays to search out harmful agents. It is found to block the formation of colon cancer and may prevent other types."

Mrs. Grieves tells us that mixing cloves and honey with it is great for rheumatism. This is understandable as rheumatism has been connected to parasites and Cloves can be used for that purpose. But of itself, Garlic can handle parasites too. Hanna uses it for Amoeba, a single cell parasite.

I have a friend that has epilepsy so I was surprised when I read in Mrs. Grieves book, "An infusion of the bruised bulbs, given before and after every meal, has been considered a good effect in epilepsy." The funny thing is that my friend, Annie, didn't want to get the flu this winter so she was eating so much garlic no one wanted to be around her. We didn't know it was keeping her healthy in more ways than one. We did find out that eating parsley after garlic or onion would deodorize the mouth. Dr. Christopher used to chew on cloves for this reason as he ate a lot of garlic.

Dr. Christopher mentioned that you can walk on a freshly cut cayenne pepper and nothing will happen to your feet but if you walk on freshly cut garlic, you will get blisters.

Hanna mentions that Garlic regulates blood pressure.

Onions and leeks have similar properties but nowhere near as strong as Garlic.

* * *

Ginseng

My sister, Donna and I started growing this in my back yard many years ago. Then we transferred them from a covered frame to a wooded area and have watched them grow, flower, and put the seeds out. Whenever she is in the area, she has to check on "her" Ginseng.

Last year we harvested one of the larger plants and Donna made tincture out of it. We have used that tincture when we need an energy boost. Donna wanted to get rid of her soda habit so she started to take Ginseng capsules and found that it helped her "make it through her day."

We, (she and I) went to a Ginseng farm in middle Wisconsin to talk to the grower. It was surprising to learn what might be on the market, as Siberian Ginseng grows here. It seems that Ginseng is a major exported commodity. People from the Orient come to Wisconsin to bid on dried roots every year.

It takes 4 or 5 years to grow Ginseng. The grower took us to his fields. They are covered with a wood lattice about 5 or 6 feet off the ground. These are rolled back for the winter but in the spring and summer they

The Simplicity of Herbal Health

cover acres of land. The grower that we visited rotated his land. Each year he harvested an acre and planted a new one, never putting Ginseng on a field that grew it before. He also showed us what he does when infection sets into a field. By pulling the lattice back in a small area, the sun burns the plants out of that area and the rest of the field stays healthy.

Ginseng is considered an adaptogen. According to Christopher Hobbs, " Until about fifty years ago, doctors commonly prescribed medicine known as roborants (which strengthen the body), tonics (which restore normal tone to tissue), and alternatives (which improve the process of nutrition and repair). What we now call adaptogens combine at least some of the major functions of roborants, tonics, and alternatives.

"Ginseng has a long-standing reputation as an anti-aging and anti-senility remedy." With the rise of Alzheimer's in the United State alone, this is one herb that might be a necessity. But we spend millions, if not billions of dollars to look younger so this might be a way to do it. Hobbs mentioned that "This is perhaps true, based on its proven ability (at least in animals) to increase the production of various hormones, enhance nerve regeneration and a number of other effects." He also mentioned that it enhances "hormonal fires" in older people. Viagra look out!

Ginseng was a wild plant in our northern states. It was found in woods but was over harvested and has since become an endangered species. We have now gone full circle and are coming back to respecting this planet and everything on it.

It is unlawful for anyone to harvest Ginseng until after the red berries have fallen. I believe there is a set date for this but I don't have that information at this time.

When you read about Ginseng, you will find that there are many cousins in this family; American Ginseng, Korean Ginseng, Red, Siberian, Chinese but after talking to the grower, I would not be surprised if a lot of these different kinds were bid for in a middle Wisconsin market.

* * *

Goldenseal

Each year the Master's Class from the School of Natural Healing has a different class herb and Goldenseal was the herb for my class. I have never studied it because it was so over used and endangered. So we will learn more about it here. Let's find out why everyone wanted to use Goldenseal.

One of the first things that I have learned about it is that it is very good to use against bacteria. It will handle E-Coli, Salmonella and Staph (the kind that creates pneumonia.) Well, we could stop here. That is more than enough for one herb to do.

Stephen Buhner tells us that it is "Active against: Staphylococcus aureus. A primary constituent of Goldenseal, berberine, has been found active in vitro against Vibrio cholerae, Streptococcus, pyogenes, Shigella SPP., Candida albicans, Escherichia coli, Klebsiella pneumoniae, Salmonella typhimurium and S. paratyphi, Corynebacterium diphtheriae, tuberculosis, Giardia lamblia and Trichomonas vaginalis, among many others."

With Berberine as the focusing factor, one might conclude that it would be very helpful for the liver as well as all of the things mentioned above.

Stephen Buhner also mentions that the FDA (Food and Drug Association) reports exaggerated the side effects of this plant, but that is their job. I think where people get into trouble with herbs is expecting them to be like drugs. The "more is better" attitude is a trademark of this.

Buhner did mention that in China, Goldenseal is not recommended for people who have very dry skin or are thin as it does have a drying effect. Perhaps this is why I have not gotten overly interested in Goldenseal.

But for infections "from top to bottom" there is nothing better.

* * *

Horsetail Grass

We will be talking more about this herb later, due to Horsetail's high silica content. David Christopher talked about Horsetail and the fact that we can't absorb silica from sand like plants can. (Remember in Chapter I, Penny Kelly told us how they do this?) David mentioned that people with high silica in their blood, mend bones faster than people with high Calcium in their blood.

Dr. Christopher has a formula that has little calcium in it but it is high in silica. It contains Horsetail as one of the ingredients and it is used to balance the calcium in the system. We all have more calcium than we need but we don't have the trace minerals that make our calcium usable, Horsetail has these trace minerals.

Here is a plant that will supply all the silica that is needed not only for bone repair but to stop bleeding in the stomach or intestinal track. It has been known to tone and heal in regard to incontinence and bed-wetting.

When one sees this plant, with its hard exterior, it isn't hard to imagine that it can give our cells support. Native Americans have used the outside of this herb to scour pots.

* * *

Lemon Balm

Here is another gem of an herb and it is growing in my garden. I wouldn't be without it. I have it growing in a raised bed that is 4 feet by 8 feet because, like all mints, they tend to travel if not contained. Her botanical name is Melissa officinalis so we call her Melissa.

Usually Lemon Balm lives on one half of this garden, but this year it took over the entire 4 X 8. When I saw what was happening, I allowed it because sometimes plants know more than we do. I remember telling a couple of friends that this was going to be the "year of virus."

Lemon Balm is anti-viral, and does this in a very nice manner. She tastes lemony and mild but really packs a whoop. In Germany, the Commission E (the equivalent of our FDA) has allowed it to be used for Herpes, a virus that is supposed to be indestructible. Yesterday I saw a lady with a cold sore and remembered when I used to get them all the time. That was before I was always nibbling on the Lemon Balm from my garden. Dr. Tyler talks about its use for cold sores but it can be used for any variety of the viruses. Did you know that there are 19 identified Herpes virus? It also has antibacterial properties.

My girlfriend came to my house with a virus. She works in an office in a cubical and had been chewing on Garlic, another antiviral herb. Her co-workers told her that if she came to work one more time smelling like garlic, they were going to send her home. So I gave her a bouquet of Lemon Balm to put in a vase on her desk and told her to chew on the leaves, and when these were gone, to come back and get some more.

Lemon Balm adds flavor to a lot of foods too. So you can be feeding your family something that will keep them a bit healthier.

Dr. Duke tells us that it is wonderful for Hypothyroidism. Many people have this condition due to the fluoride that is put into our drinking water. He does suggest Lemon Balm for the thyroid along with a few other herbs but what I liked best was that in his explanation he says, "…Because they seem to have the ability to normalize thyroid hormone levels regardless of whether there's too much or too little." People always want to know if I had Hypo or Hyperthyroid. It doesn't make any difference. The organ was sick. When we give the body the building blocks to heal, it does. Isn't that exciting?

Melissa is so easy to grow and I can't think of a reason not to have some of it around.

* * *

Mullein

Hanging in one of my rooms, I have an Indian ceremonial pipe. I packed it with powdered Mullein leaf to smoke at a women's ceremony that was held at my home. This is not a new idea. Native American's smoked mullein to assist with lung problems. For years we have been telling everyone that smoking is bad for the lungs but getting the powder of Mullein into the lungs, can be healing for them.

Dr. Christopher talked about Mullein as being great for healing glands. In Chapter II, I talked about healing my Thyroid with it in the formula that Dr. Christopher created, 3 parts Mullein and 1 part Lobelia. This formula was to clean out the lymph glands but works for all glands.

The Simplicity of Herbal Health

Mullein has been known as "Camper's toilet paper" because the leaves are very large and soft, sometimes as large as two feet. Even though the leaves have a soft hairiness to them, I would use a leaf from this plant as an emergency bandage.

Fomentations have been made from these leaves by adding hot vinegar and water to apply in cases of "inflamed piles, ulcers, tumours, mumps, acute inflammation of the tonsils, malignant sore throat, dropsy (water retention) of the joints, sciatica, spinal tenderness, etc." according to Hutchens.

Mullein has also been used to handle hemorrhoids and as a tea it is great for the kidneys.

The top of the second year plant looks like a candle with its long flower head towering as much as a foot to three feet higher than the leaf part, bringing this plant up to 7 or even 10 feet tall at times. The flowers open a few at a time in different places up and down this flower head. These flowers have been used for ear problems by putting them into a small jar and filling it with good oil such as olive oil. The flowers add their bit to the ointment and allow this to heal and soothe the ears.

I would think that these second year plants would make a wonderful torch when semi-dried to use at night. I will have to check this out sometime.

Mullein is a two-year plant so it needs to be re-seeded. This can be done by tipping the flower heads and taking the seeds out for later use. I always have one or two in both stages of life growing in my flower gardens.

A lot of these herbs get really big but they add so much to the variation of a garden. Why would we grow only 5 different kinds of plants in our gardens? We need to create an orchestra of plants. Why just have all brass or all woodwinds, instead create a mixture of different harmonies.

Let Mullein be one of your new plants. And remember that the second year it is going to get 4 to 10 feet tall so perhaps you would like it in the back of the your garden.

Phyllis Heitkamp Master Herbalist

* * *

Sage

My Cousin, Gloria did her Master's thesis on Sage. To help her, I went into Dr. Duke's database and was " blown out of the water" by all the things this wonderful little plant is capable of doing. He had about 25 pages of things that this plant could do. So where do I start?

Sage lightens the teeth when the leaves are rubbed on them, according to Gloria. She mentioned that when she was taking a lot of herbal extracts, her teeth got very dark so she rubbed a sage leaf on them and to her surprise, the leaf took on the coloration by pulling it away from her teeth. As a side note, she mentioned using glycerin extracts tend to soften the teeth.

I am always amazed at how these herbs work and what you can use them for. It is easy to understand the fact that this is a lifetime study.

Stephen Buhner says that it is another antibiotic, along with being astringent, antiseptic, diaphoretic, tonic and expectorant.

Buhner tells us that it is active against Strep, Staph, E-coli, Candida albicans, Salmonella and many of the different kinds of lung infections.

Duke's database tells of properties in Sage that are: "Anti-malarial, Cancer- preventive, Antiviral, Paraciticide, Pesticide, and anti-inflammatory." From this you can tell that we are talking about another heavy-duty plant.

Hanna Kroeger suggests using Sage on a piece of buttered wholegrain bread for allergies in general. She suggests eating it or drinking Sage tea for mouth blisters. For bloating, Hanna suggests combining it with Peppermint as Sage also aids in protein digestion. Hanna felt that drinking Sage tea would be helpful for memory as well as glandular weakness. It can also be rubbed on insect bites. A Sage tea gargle is wonderful for a sore throat.

The aromatic oil contained in sage makes it wonderful for a stuffy head. By putting a bundle of cut sage in a hot bath, the sinuses unplug nicely.

After all these wonderful things about Sage, Dr. Tyler cautions us by saying that the volatile oil in this herb has not been fully tested for safety. He does go on to tell us that the German Commission E has approved both internal and external use of it but wants us to not overuse Sage.

Another caution or bit of information that I would like to extend is the fact that nursing mothers should not use sage until it is time to wean the baby. Sage will dry up milk production.

Sage has been used ceremoniously for hundreds of years by Native Americans to cleanse not only their area but to cleanse themselves of negative energy. The smudging with sage was well known before major events were to take place.

When I was in Utah taking my Master's exam, a group of us found wild Sage in the mountains that we were in. We bundled it up to use it to do a purification ceremony before we took our exam.

There are many different ways to look at plant beings. Native Americans revered them.

* * *

Slippery Elm

One of my "Big Guns" (herbs that seem to do everything) is Slippery Elm Bark. This inner bark is so healing. Let me tell you about Slippery Elm Bark. One of the first things that I do is allow my students to taste Slippery Elm Bark powder. (Bark can be powdered by putting the dried pieces in a coffee grinder.) Then I ask them what it tastes like. They all recognize the taste but not everyone makes the connection. It tastes like maple syrup because it contains the sap or blood of another tree. A lot of tree saps have this taste.

I have read where Native American's would cut a slice of bark from almost any tree and apply it to a wound by putting the inner bark against the affected area, then they would tie it on and continue with what they were doing.

According to Alma Hutchens in her book, <u>Indian Herbology of North American</u>, Slippery Elm has the nutrient value of Oatmeal. For this reason, when we find that a person who has been unable to gain weight or just hold onto weight, such as a small baby or a very old person, Slippery Elm gruel is given as food and they are able to assimilate the nutrients readily.

Mixing water with Slippery Elm powder makes this gruel. Using a pile of powdered herb, an indentation is made in the top of the pile. A little water is dropped into this indentation and the water is moved around until a small bead of Slippery Elm powder is created. To this bead, a little more water is added and the bead is moved around and enlarges. This is continued until all of the Slippery Elm powder is in the bead and then water is added until you get the consistency that is just right for the situation, in this case, a gruel. It is a bland food and therefore makes it good when the subject isn't interested in food. It is soothing to the stomach when other foods are rejected. It is also great as a baby food at weaning time.

This same method is used to make a paste when applying this to burns, wounds, and other skin problems. Burns need all of Slippery Elm's nutrition to rebuild deep layers of tissue. If we just handle the burn for infections, where are the building blocks coming from to rebuild the area? This is not to say that we overlook that possibility of infection but in the 50 constituents that Dr. James Duke lists in his database for Slippery Elm, many of them have antibacterial properties.

Dr. Christopher suggested making this paste and applying it to knees and hips that need to be rebuilt. He said that anyone with a bad knee or bad hip has no business running around, so by putting this paste on the area and reapplying it as the body uses it up (And it does absorb it through the skin), one can rebuild a knee or hip without surgery.

According to the GlobalherbV2.0 Data base: Slippery Elm Bark can be used for Diarrhea, Inflammation, Wounds, Sore Throats, Burns, Bronchitis, Congestion, Coughs, Tumors-uterus, Colitis, Constipation, Crohns Disease, Gangrene, Gastritis, Hemorrhoids, Swollen Lymph Glands, Tuberculosis (Consumption), Ulcers (Gastric or skin), Acne, Appendicitis, Asthma, Broken Bones, Bruises, Chapped Skin, Croup, Diaper Rash, Diarrhea, Diphtheria, Diverticulitis, Heart burn, Hiatus Hernia, Infection, Irritable Bowel Syndrome, Lung Hemorrhage, Nausea, Poison Ivy, Rash, Swelling, Typhoid Fever, Wasting disease, and Worms.

The Simplicity of Herbal Health

That seems to be a lot but in Dr. Duke's database I found Antiatherosclerotic, and anti-asthmatic as additional properties. Also there were Anticatarac and candidicide properties listed.

I guess with all of that, you can see why Slippery Elm is one of my "Big Guns".

I used it to clean up my mother's leg when it was black from her toes to her knee. She had rubbed the top of her foot until she had two ulcerated sores about ½ inch deep and no one mentioned the sores until the leg turned black.

So using the Slippery Elm Bark in tea form, we wrapped her leg with cotton strips and saturated the cotton. We put a towel and plastic under all of this so the liquid would not run all over. Keeping this tea slightly warm but not hot, we continued to saturate the leg. Within four days, the all-black leg had turned purple with pink strips in it. We treated the ulcerated sores with a salve that would not be washed away by the tea. In the next few days the leg got pinker and pinker until all that was left were the sores that had scabbed over. They took another week to fall off and the leg was back to normal.

Many singers carry Slippery Elm lozenges to soothe their throats that might get overworked or inflamed. It speeds the healing process by coating the area with tissue-strengthening properties.

* * *

Willow

Here is an herb that has long been used for pain. The salicylic acid in this plant is the forerunner of aspirin. When using Willow bark one was using the buffered acid but when the chemists extracted the "active ingredient", it was found that this was too strong for the human body.

In her book, Barbara Griggs mentions the process of duplicating the effects that herbs can do by making a drug out of the parts. She says, " In regular medical practice, one of the great drawbacks to the use of plant drugs has always been the difficulty of producing anything like a standard dose. The old herbalists, it turned out, have been absolutely right when they insisted that a particular plant had to be gathered not only at a certain time of the year, but even at a certain time of the day or night." We talked a little about this in the beginning of this chapter.

Dr. Tyler tells us that the amount of active ingredient in Willow is not enough to handle pain. What was it that I read in another book…that maybe on paper these things are not possible but thousands of years of use, say that they work.

Willow bark has been used for a very long time for muscle aches and pains, for headaches and to help with arthritis.

* * *

Yarrow

When the systems of the body need to be stimulated into working, Yarrow is called for. Dr. Christopher used it to stimulate the blood when the body was having a problem. I have used it for this purpose and seen results over night.

Yarrow has many more wonderful properties that have the "ability to keep up the strength and act as a blood cleanser, at the same time opening the pores to permit free perspiration, taking along with it unwanted waste and relieving the kidneys.." according to Hutchens.

Hutchens also suggested chewing on a leaf when troubled by a toothache.

The American Indians used Yarrow for skin wounds and according to Hutchens, the oil or decoction of Yarrow will prevent the hair from falling out if taken internally and applied to the scalp.

Dr. Christopher went one better on this last idea. He said that if you use a rinse of Yarrow tea after shampooing the hair, the hair would, after a little time, return to the color that it was when you were a teenager. If you find that this works, please let me know.

* * *

I have tried to cover some of the herbs on this "walk" that haven't been talked about in other chapters. There are so many more.

I have found that every herbalist has 100 to 200 favorite herbs and each herbalist's favorites are a bit different. When something for a particular problem in the body is mentioned, I stop and think, "Why not? These herbs are so versatile that they can handle more than one thing." I hope that you have enjoyed meeting some of my friends and are ready to put them to work for you and your family.

Standardization

I would be very remiss if I didn't mention standardization, the process of standardizing herbs. Dr. Duke and I disagree on this subject, as he pointed out, when he goes to a health food store, he doesn't know how long that bottle of herbs has been on the shelf. When it is standardized, he knows that at least the active ingredient is still there.

I would rather see each person learning to create their own medicine, much like canning tomatoes for the winter, harvest your own herbs. When I see chemicals added to herbs and then be labeled as that herb, I get very upset. When you have a recipe for a cake and you put more flour or more eggs in than the recipe calls for, you don't have the same product. When you put more of one active ingredient into a capsule of herbs and call it a standardized herb, you don't have the same product.

What do you have? A drug, complete with all the side effects that are being shown on drug commercials. Wholesome is healthy. Part-some is unbalanced.

Herbs have proven themselves true as wholesome health care during the past few thousands of years. Have they changed? Yes, they have evolved just as we and everything else on this planet has changed. But the recipe that makes them whole is still in place from the original designer. Perhaps if it should be changed, HE should be doing the changing instead of our chemists?

Chapter IV - Resources

Batmanghelidy MD, F., *Your Body's Many Cries for Water,* Global Health Solutions, Falls Church, VA. 1992, 181 pg.

Blake, Steven, <u>Global Herb-Version 3.0</u>, *California, 1995*

Bremness, Lesley, *Herbs*, Dorling Kindersley, NY, 1994, 304 pg.

Buhner, Stephen Harrold, *Herbal Antibiotics,* Storey publishing, North Adams, MA.,1999, 135 pg.

Carson, Rachel, *Silent Spring,* The Riverside Press, Cambridge, MA, 1962, 355 pg.

Christopher, John R., ND, M.H., *Regenerative Diet,* Christopher Publications, Springville, UT, 1982, 275 pg., 1-800-372-8255

Christopher, John R, ND, M.H., *School of Natural Healing*, Christopher Publications, Springville, UT, 1976, 724 pg., <u>www.snh.cc</u>

Crow, Tis Mal, *Native Plants Native Healing - Traditional Muskogee Way,* Native Voices, Summertown, TN., 2001, 143 pg.

Culpeper, Nicholas, *Culpeper's Complete Herbal & English Physician,* Meyerbooks Glenwood, IL., 1990, 402 pg.

Duke, James A., Ph.D., <u>Dr. Duke's Phytochemical and Ethnobotanical Database,</u> 2003

Foster/Duke, *Peterson's Field Guides/ Medicinal Plants*, Houghton Mifflin Co., New York, NY., 1990, 244 pg..

Foster, Steven, *Herbal Renaissance,* Peregrine Smith Books, Layton, UT, 1997, 234 pg.

Grieves, Mrs., *A Modern Herbal*, Dover Publications, Inc., New York, NY, 902 pg.

Griggs, Barbara, *Green Pharmacy,* Healing Arts Press, Rochester, VT, 1991, 379 pg.

Hobbs, Christopher, L.Ac., *Stress & Natural Healing,* Interweave Press, Inc. Loveland, CO, 1997, 240 pg.

Hutchens, Alma R., *Indian Herbology of North American*, Shambhala, Boston, MA,1991, 382 pages.

Kelly, Penny, *Robes-A Book of Coming Changes*, Authors Choice Press. Lincoln, NE, 1999, 318 pg.

Kroeger, Hanna Rev., *Heal Your Life With Home Remedies And Herbs,* Hay House, Inc., Carlsbad, CA, 1998, 296 pg.

From *The Merck Manual of Medical Information – Home Edition,* p. 1509, edited by Mark H Beers and Robert Berkow. Copyright 1997 by Merck & Co., Inc., Whitehousen Station, NJ.

National Audubon Society Field Guide to North American Wildflowers, Chanticleer Press, Inc., New York, NY, 887 pages

Ritchason, Jack, N.D., *The little Herb Encyclopedia*, Woodland Health Books, Pleasant Grove, UT, 1995, 402 pages

Toffler, Alvin, *The Third Wave,* William Morrow and Company, Inc., NY., 1980, 544 pg

Tyler, Ph.D., Varro E., *Herbs of Choice*, Pharmaceutical Products Press, New York, NY 209 pages

Werback, M., *Healing With Foods,* (Note- Check Dukes Database for WER)

Wright, Machaelle Small, *Behaving As If The God In All Life Mattered*, Perelandra, Ltd., Warrenton, VA., 1983, 270 pg

Wright, Machaelle Small, *Perelandra Garden Workbook, Second Edition*, Perelandra, Ltd., Warrenton, VA, 1987, 328 pg

Chapter V
Another Wonderful Tea

The first thing that we are going to do before settling down to study this chapter is have a cup of tea. Today I wish to suggest Nettle tea. This can be fresh, dried or in tea bags from your local health food store.

Nettle is one of my favorites, that is, if I have a favorite. There are so many that I like but a nice mellow Nettle tea is so comforting from time to time.

Nettle is loaded with minerals. Dr. Duke found about 70 constituents and so many of them were hard working. He mentioned properties with the ability to be: Fungicide, antioxidants, antibacterial…some were vasodilators. (They open the veins a little to allow more blood to flow) One thing that he mentioned in his research and it comes from his <u>Economic and Medical Plant Research. 1:53</u>, was that the Linoleic Acid is antifibrinolytic. This means that it, as Dr. Shook said, "…is nature's masterpiece solvent of fibrin." The body sometimes creates fibrin to web things together. In some cases these fibers need to be dissolved and are not, due to one thing or another. Nettle, according to Dr. Edward E. Shook, is one of two wonderful herbs that will dissolve fibers. This is one reason among many for having a cup of this tea.

Nettle is a small plant, about 2 to 4 feet tall, with alternate long leaves that have saw-teeth edges to them. On the edge of these leaves and stems are tiny hairs that will leave one's skin stinging for a while. This stinging property was used by Native Americans to bring blood to an area that needed healing. Most people shy away from the plant for this reason but the spine of the leaf contains an antidote to the burning. When the plant has been dried or cooked, the stinging is not there.

The juice in the spine of the leaves has wonderful properties and will counteract the poison of other plants as well, such as Poison Ivy or Poison Oak.

A friend came to me with large blisters on his foot and up his leg to the knee. He told me that it was Poison Ivy. I told him that he should make a tea of stinging Nettle and bathe that area in it. He called me later that day

Phyllis Heitkamp Master Herbalist

and was pleased because the blisters went down quickly. This should tell us that Nettle is great at cleaning up poisons. In Duke's database I bumped into a property in this plant that does just that, it cleans up abnormal function in the intestines too, another great reason for starting this chapter with a cup of Nettle tea.

If you are interested in more information about Nettle, I wrote a bit more about it in <u>Wisconsin Medicinal Herbs</u>.

The Simplicity of Herbal Health

Kidneys

We want to talk about kidneys here and it is interesting that yesterday I was talking to an acupuncturist who mentioned that the kidney area, along with the lower back, relates to fear in Eastern Healing. When I think about the times that my lower back has given me trouble, this made sense.

Hanna Kroeger mentioned that metals collect in the right kidney. She has an herbal product called *Metaline*. It contains Pumpkin seed, Okra, Rhubarb Root, Capsicum, Peppermint and Dulse.

She also talked about the left kidney as the collector of infections.

Parsley is an herb that we grow in the garden or find on our plates when we eat in restaurants, but few of us really eat it. It is great for the kidneys.

I have many reservations about Dr. Varro E. Tyler's work because everything I read from him is doomsday, so with reservation, I will mention that regarding Parsley, he is in true form. He talks about the fact that pregnant women and fair skinned people should not eat Parsley. He is taking two properties and thinking that they are what Parsley is all about. But one has to remember that he was a "Lilly Distinguished Professor of Pharmacognosy at Purdue" This means that the chemical companies loved him. In reference to his statement regarding people who should not eat parsley, he does say that they would have to eat an "Average daily dose is 6 g. Many times this amount is consumed by persons who enjoy the Lebanese salad Tabbouleh." But this is his quote?

Dr. Jack Ritchason says, "Parsley can be used during pregnancy, but not in high doses, as it tends to induce labor pains. Parsley has a drying up effect on mother's milk and can be used to help in the weaning process."

Over three hundred years ago, a nun in Germany, Hildegard of Bingen, recommended Parsley in wine for pains of the heart and spleen.

Here we have an herb that is high in chlorophyll, making it wonderful for the breath as well as the blood. It is very high in iron, more so than a lot of other greens and mineral-rich in most other nutrients.

Parsley is wonderful for the kidneys. The Root of the parsley has been used for stones in the kidney area and also to treat liver problems. Culpeper, noted herbalist, felt that parsley was the herb of choice for treatment of kidney and bladder problems.

Herbs aren't just for people. Animals have used them with and without our help forever. Parsley is no exception. My friend, Carol, called to tell me that one of her cats was having a kidney problem and wanted to know what would be helpful. I suggested that she float some crushed parsley in the cat's drinking water. It would not hurt the healthy cat either. After her cat was doing well, she called to tell me that her cats won't drink out of their water bowl without the parsley in it.

While we are talking about animals, let's put the animal dosages here. When using tablets or capsules, plan the dose by body weight, using:

1/4 the human dose for a cat
1/2 the human dose for a small dog
3/4 the human dose for a medium sized dog
A full adult human dose for a large dog
A full adult human dose for very large pets – horses.

With Homeopathic Dosages for pets
Same as the herbal dosages

With Flower Remedies
As stated on the container

Getting back to herbs that are good for the Kidneys: an herb that is a good diuretic is one we talked about earlier in this book, Burdock. Those big leaves can be made into a tea or eaten in a salad and they will help the kidneys move fluid out of the body.

Now we are talking about something that has been used for a very long time in America to soothe the kidneys and stabilize the urinary tract. Juniper Berries are usually found in combination with other herbs for this purpose. Marshmallow root is one that I would add to this combination. Black Cohosh root is another plant that is used in combination with Juniper Berries, as is Golden Seal.

The Simplicity of Herbal Health

Juniper berries are wonderful for the Kidneys. When I first heard this, I went to my Juniper bush and collected the berries and then I read that it isn't the berries that were grown this year but the very black ones from last year that are to be used. The blue ones that grew this year need to be left on the bush for another season.

I remember hearing Dr. Christopher talk about Juniper and he mentioned a specific kind called Juniper monosperma. This means that the berry has one seed in it. When checking with Dr. Duke after I couldn't find Monosperma in his database, he sent me information on all the Junipers from Juniperus bermudiana (for warts), Juniperus communis; which is good for everything from arteriosclerosis to bronchitis and on to being good for the kidneys and the stomach. When he wrote about Monosperma, the reference was for asthma, congestion, arthritis, stiffness but nothing about it being good for the kidneys. So I was still wondering about the information that Dr. Christopher had given us. I called a fellow student and she remembers him making the reference to Monosperma also. Well, I guess it was just a slip that was made because the Christopher product for kidneys called *KB* uses Juniperus communis.

Hanna mentioned that one could boil a handful of cut Juniper branches in water for 30 minutes. This tea is antibacterial and is used externally only.

Queen of the Meadow (Gravel Root or Joe Pye) along with Uva Ursa (Bearberry) are very helpful in dissolving stones.

When we are working with stones in the kidney area, there are two herbs that are wonderful for this purpose. One is Hydrangea Root and the other is Gravel Root. These two guys specialize in dissolving stones. Blue Moon label puts out a three-herb combination, the third herb being Marshmallow Root and this combination will take care of stones in 24 hours. So many people have used this combination and gotten relief quickly. My nephew Douglas, after taking this combination for his stones, wanted to know where he could get more because he had friends who are dealing with kidney stones.

I have often wondered when they do sound therapy on Kidney stones what really happens? When you play marbles and you hit the marble in the center of the circle with yours, the marble that is hit will be sent flying in one direction or another. When a kidney stone is hit by sound waves to be broken, where do the little pieces go? Dr. Christopher talked about the quantity of tubing in the kidneys and how very fragile they are, that they can be damaged with a fingernail, even cut in two this way.

Perhaps that is why Blue Moon puts Marshmallow in its combination. Marshmallow is such a wonderful herb. It is so healing. And it will tackle old as well as new wounds. After a stone, which is a calcium snowflake, has damaged the tubes in the kidneys, one needs a "big Gun" healer to come in and "fix" it up.

Marshmallow belongs to the Malva family and this family is wonderful. It has a talent for cleaning up very old wounds. According to Dr. Tyler, the German Kommission E (the equivalent of our Food and Drug Association) has declared all of the malvas to be effective demulcents. This means that they have a soothing and softening quality about them. In addition to this is the fact that they help with poisons and pain.

Dr. Christopher mentioned that this family could be used to clean up gangrene. I decided to test this when my Mother's leg was black. My sister, Betty had been checking on Mom while I was on vacation and called to tell me that Mom had two very deep ulcerated sores on the top of her foot and her leg was black from toes to knee. Mother was in a wheelchair due to the stroke that she had a year earlier. She didn't get a lot of circulation and had rubbed sores on the top of her foot from the bed railing at night.

I remembered what Dr. Christopher said about using common malva to handle this kind of problem. His method was to fill a bucket with hands full of malva and pour hot water over it. When the water has cooled enough for anyone to put an arm in, then the person who has the gangrene, would put their limb into the water for 20 minutes. After that time, switch to cool water for 10 minutes while the caregiver gathers another hand full of common malva to start over. This can take all day.

Because of the circumstances, I decided that I would have to formulate another way to do this. I sent my sister to my house to get some Marshmallow and Slippery Elm. I had her make some Marshmallow Tea and some Slippery Elm paste. She was to put the Slippery Elm into the ulcerated sores and then wrap the leg with cotton material. (I like to keep cotton dishtowels or diapers around.) I suggested elevating Mom's leg and putting plastic under it, then wetting the cotton wrap with the Marshmallow

The Simplicity of Herbal Health

Tea, keeping it wet with the tea, checking the sores periodically and adding more Slippery Elm as needed.

I returned four days later and found that the ulcerated sores had scabbed over and were healing nicely, so it was time to apply the *Complete Tissue Formula (BF&C)*. The leg was purple with pink strips when I first saw it although my sister told me that it had been very black. In a week, the leg was all pink and within two weeks the scabs fell off from the sores.

Mother lived with a caregiver. We had an agreement that if anything happened to Mom, she would call one of the daughters before she contacted the medical profession. One of the caregiver's sons threatened to turn us into the authorities, as he didn't feel that we were taking proper care of Mother. I asked him if he would give me two weeks and then do that. After Mom was well, the caregiver asked if I would help her girlfriend, who had black toes. I told her that would be easy and then I found out that her girlfriend was in the hospital. I can't help anyone in a hospital. The girlfriend lost her toes when the doctor cut them off.

The medical profession isn't taught how to handle gangrene or the putrefaction of skin, other than to cut it out. It is a lot to ask of the body to heal itself but it is very capable of doing this if given the building blocks. We are back to Dr. Christopher's original idea of the 5 things to eat (Fruits, Vegetables, Whole Grains, Nuts and Seeds), along with wonderful distilled water, lots of fresh air, and herbs. Our bodies are designed to self-heal.

I mentioned earlier about how Marshmallow helped a lady with diarrhea. I know that I would use Marshmallow on Diverticulitis. (Pockets in the intestine)

Other members of the Malva family have also been used for cleaning up old wounds. Hollyhock is a Malva family member and can be used on bedsores.

Common malva is a weed that is found just about everywhere and I have read where it can be used for Angina.

In Chapter 3, I mentioned that Hanna Kroeger used Blue Malva, another member of this family, to heal heart valves.

Phyllis Heitkamp Master Herbalist

Other things that Marshmallow has been used for are: coughs, bed wetting, nosebleeds, blood in stool or in urine, to increase or enrich breast milk, cancer, eye inflammation, hemorrhoids, kidney problems, stomach problems, swallowing difficulty, teething, tumors, ulcers, and even whooping cough according to my Globalherb program.

Globalherb suggests that for kidney infections one might use Chaparral. Remember when we talked about this one in Chapter two? Also mentioned is Plantain, another wonderful herb for drawing out the infection. Last, but not least, is Uva Ursa for Kidney infections.

Hanna Kroeger in <u>Herbal Insights Magazine, Winter 1997</u>, talked about "symptoms of kidney imbalance including poor clearance of toxins through the kidneys, water retention (I call this puffiness) urinary tract infections, mucous accumulation, coldness, rheumatic complaints, tiredness and dizziness." She suggested that we, "Eat within the seasons at our latitude." By eating things like Bananas and oranges and hot chilies or any other summer/tropical crops in the wintertime, we tend to make the elimination sluggish. There are many foods that are stored for winter in our area, mostly root vegetables along with dried foods from our Latitude.

Dr. Christopher was one for suggesting this also. He told us to "Eat from under our own fig tree."

Spring is the time to cleanse with what nature provides. So you will find a great deal of greens available early in the spring season.

Cornsilk tea is also recommended to strengthen the kidneys. Hanna suggested 3 cups per day.

Sometimes we are very hard on our kidneys by overburdening them with an excess of protein. The Soy industry has suggested that by replacing meat protein with soy protein, our kidneys would benefit, as soy doesn't produce an increased activity.

According to the Globalherb program, some of the other herbs that are helpful for the kidneys are: Nettle, Comfrey Rt., Chaparral, Calendula, Blessed Thistle, Black Cohosh, Chickweed, Dandelion, Horsetail, Barberry, Astragalus, Asparagus Rt., Sesame seeds, Sassafras, Raspberry leaves, Peppermint, Knotgrass, False Unicorn, St. John's Wort, Sheep Sorrel, Water lily, Yarrow, and Wood Betony.

The Simplicity of Herbal Health

Note: Water lily in the Globalherb list. Dr. Christopher stated that White Pond Lily "would handle incontinence." It is the bulb of this plant that does this and because it is an endangered species, one gets this material from growers.

Dr. Christopher's Herb Company has two products for this purpose. One is called *Bladder Formula* it contains: Parsley root, Juniper berries, Marshmallow Rt., White Pond Lily, Gravel Root, Uva Ursi leaves, Lobelia herb, Ginger root, and Black Cohosh root.

The second formula is directed at Children (Bed-wetters), It is called *Kid-E-Dry*. It contains: White Pond Lily, Catnip herb, Cornsilk, Hydrangea root, Lobelia herb, Parsley root, Slippery Elm bark, and natural cherry flavor made in a glycerin base.

Some of the symptoms that the kidneys need attention come from swollen ankles or what I call puffy skin. This is where the skin on our bodies seems to be fat but is the retention of water that is not being flushed out of the body.

Hanna talks about the right knee being connected to the kidneys. She suggests that if your right knee has some discomfort, do something to assist the health of the kidneys.

Hanna also gave us a formula for Stones in the kidneys:

1 quart distilled water
6 level tablespoons of Cream of Tarter
2 tablespoons of borax

Stir to dissolve
Give 3 tablespoons in a glass of water to a large person
Give 2 tablespoons in a glass of water to a small person
Morning, Noon and Night for 10 days and they are gone.
(Personal comment: 10 days is a long time)

To relieve pain while dissolving the stones, Hanna suggests.... Lay on a stairway with your head down and feet up.

Phyllis Heitkamp Master Herbalist

Our Skin

The next thing that we are going to discuss in this book has to do with skin. This is the largest organ in our body and probably the most abused.

According to Dr. Christopher, the skin is our second set of lungs. It breathes and needs to be cleaned and brushed. It likes to breathe through natural materials such as cotton, wool or silk.

Dr. Christopher suggested using his *The Complete Tissue Formula* (*BF&C*) for Dermatitis. It stood for <u>B</u>ones, <u>F</u>lesh and <u>C</u>artilage. It rebuilds skin.

When I broke my collarbone, I took the *Complete Tissue Formula*. It contains a lot of herbs to help repair and re-build, but I wanted to make sure that everything in the formula was going to be used so I added another of Dr. Christopher's formulas called the *Calcium Assimilation Formula (Calc-T)*. The second formula contains very little calcium but all the trace minerals that are needed to utilize any available calcium in my body. My clavicle healed in short order. In 4 weeks, the only things that I had to work on were the muscles that had been traumatized in the area. As an added benefit of using these formulas, my nails and hair grew really fast.

For Poison Oak or Poison Ivy he suggested Nettle. In the first part of this chapter, I talked about the man who had Poison all over his legs and used Nettle. It works well. But there are so many things that can help when you run into something like this. Look around when you get into this situation, you will find Plantain or Mullein, or Hounds Tongue or maybe Lilacs. They all have the power to neutralize these toxins.

Hanna Kroeger used to say that within a few hundred feet of wherever you are, there is help. This can be when we are in a snowstorm or flood, and maybe the help is only a log to climb on or under to wait out the problem.

* * *

One week ago I had a friend bring her 3-year-old over. This little darling was covered with hives. She had them everywhere on her body. There are a lot of plants that have antihistamine properties. In Dr. Duke's, <u>The</u>

The Simplicity of Herbal Health

<u>Green Pharmacy</u>", he talked about his son getting hives and like most of us that was BH (Before Herbs) so he used diphenhydramine (Benadryl). He said that with his present knowledge, he would go the herbal route. We all started out believing in the medical system. It is only as we learn that we change our ideas on this and that is what this book is all about.

What Duke says in the hives section of his book is, "What doctors don't say – because they generally don't know – is that many plants contain antihistamine compounds. My database is full of these plants: Camomile and wild oregano have at least 7 different antihistaminic chemicals, and rue has six. Weighing in with five we have basil, echinacea, fennel, fig, ginkgo, grapefruit, passionflower, tarragon, tea (Green or black) thyme and yarrow."

So this little girl was given Chamomile tincture with a Chamomile tea to wash it down. Her Mom told me that at first it got worse but within hours, she could see the results and by the next day, the little girl had very few spots left and wanted to go to her swimming lessons.

According to Dr. Tyler, Chamomile is a very safe herb and used mostly for stomach or intestinal complaints. He also mentions that in present-day Europe it is used in skin creams and lotions for "skin irritations, including those caused by bacterial infections."

Here is a wonderful herb that is very easy to grow. According to Steven Foster, "In Boulder, Colorado, you can find the plant naturalized along roadsides and in the cracks of sidewalks, where seeds have "escaped" from Celestial Seasonings." (The National Tea Company.)

It is the flower head that is most useful in making the tea of this plant. So when growing it you needn't tear up the whole plant but use the flowers as they open. These can be dried as suggested in Chapter IV for later use.

Chamomile has, for the most part, been associated with its soothing and sedative qualities but it has some powerful properties. Dr. Tyler has been quoted as saying that "the Germans describe it as *'alles zutraut'* –capable of anything." This makes it a wonderful nervine. Check Chapter III to find out how nervines work.

According to Dr. Ritchason, Chamomile has been used for: Abscesses, Anxiety, Asthma, Bladder problems, Bronchitis, Calluses, Circulation (poor), Colds, Colic, Colitis, Constipation, Corns, Cramps (menstrual), Dandruff, Diarrhea, Diverticulitis, Drug addiction, Earache, Eyes (sore), Fever, Flu, Gallstones, Gangrenous sores, and to expel Gas.

* * *

For itching skin, Dr. Christopher reminds us that any itching is caused from a toxic condition. One of the things that he recommends is an Apple Cider Vinegar wash.

Another wonderful herb that I like for itching is Chickweed. Chickweed grows everywhere and is in everyone's garden.

When I had Shingles, I sent my husband out to get two handfuls of chickweed from under our oak tree. After sorting out the other weeds, I put the chickweed into a pan on the stove with just enough water to cover it. I simmered it for about 15 minutes and then allowed it to cool. This was a long wait, as any of you know who have had Shingles. Then I applied this tea to my skin with a cloth. The relief was immediate. The itching stopped. I think I remember letting out a very large sigh.

That only handles the symptoms of Shingles. For more information on Shingles check Chapter III.

Chickweed is a wonderful herb and it has such a mild taste.

While at a function held on an organic farm, an intern came running into the barn to get me. It seems that one of the guests had left his soda sitting out. When he went to drink from it, he swallowed a hornet and was stung inside the esophagus. We went to the garden and I pulled up some Chickweed along with a leaf of Plantain. I gave them to the guest and told him to chew on them, swallowing only the juice. I went to my car and got some Capsicum and put it into a little water. When I came back, I told him to spit out the herbs and sip on the water. He did. I left him with instructions that if he found that he had any trouble swallowing or taking a deep breath, he should go to town to the emergency room of the local hospital.

I inquired at the farm later as to how the gentleman was doing but no one seemed to know. They gave me his phone number and I called him.

The Simplicity of Herbal Health

He was very upset with me but was only angry about the capsicum. This could have been very serious and to have him angry only because the capsicum "burned" his throat made me laugh. Both the Chickweed and the Plantain have the ability to pull the toxins out of the area. The capsicum would bring the blood to clean up the rest.

Chickweed will do this to mosquito bites too. I have seen the bites bathed in Chickweed tea and the itching stops immediately, the residue from the bites disappear within a few hours.

I have even suggested it to a mother whose infant child was covered with eczema. Dr. Christopher was used to women nursing their children so he suggested that the nursing mother drink gallons of Chickweed tea. I suggested that the mother bath this child in chickweed tea a couple of times a day, because she wasn't nursing. For adults with eczema, Dr. Christopher suggested three to four cups of this tea and the chickweed bath.

Herbal baths are fun and relaxing. An easy way to do this is to bundle the herbs and tie them together, allowing them to float on the bath water. Or make a tea bag out of a cotton sock and filled with the herb of choice. Then we run hot water into the tub and hop in to a tea bath. When we don't have it growing in our back yards, the next best thing is to uses many tea bags from the store.

Chickweed is so wonderful at pulling things out of the body that it will grab fat in the body and take it out. For this reason, one can find this herb in a lot of herbal weight loss products.

* * *

The next herb that is so wonderful for the skin is Slippery Elm. (See Chapter IV) This is the inner bark of the Elm tree. It is slippery because it creates a gummy mucilaginous substance. This makes it a great herb to apply to wounds or ulcers.

I got a call one morning from an upset person who told me that she had some acreage and had done a burn on the back section of it. When she used her rake to control it, particles of burning debris landed on her arm, burning an 8 to 10 inch section of her arm.

Phyllis Heitkamp Master Herbalist

This happened 10 days earlier and in the meantime she had followed through with what she thought would be the right thing to do, she went to the doctor. He cleaned it out, put a chemical healer on it and told her to come back in 10 days. She had just returned from the second time at the doctor and called a nurse friend of hers. She was crying and said that she couldn't do that again. They had done a debridement ("Surgical removal of dead or contaminated tissue and foreign matter from a wound" – American Heritage College Dictionary – Third Edition) They had removed the 10 day old scabs that had formed on top of the burned area. This is standard practice for handling burns, I have learned. Why do you think scabs form? When the body is healing why would you interfere? Why not assist?

The Nurse that she called suggested that she call me. The Nurse had taken my classes.

I told this very upset lady that she might put a poultice of Slippery Elm bark on her burns. Slippery Elm would rebuild the flesh that had been burned away. I suggested some Marshmallow root tea to be washed over this area also. I asked her to call me later in the day after she had done this.

I got a call about 6:00 in the evening and she wanted to know what she should do next. I told her to continue to add the Slippery Elm as the body in its rebuilding process uses it up. She wanted to know if she should add more bark to what was already on her arm. In talking with her, I found out that she had used cut product instead of powered Slippery Elm. These bark chunks were sitting on this raw meat. I told her to fill her sink with room temperature water and soak the bark off. Do not pull it off. When it was all off she was to come to my house.

When she arrived I made a poultice out of Slippery Elm powder. Slippery Elm doesn't like to mix with water easily so we made a small pile of powder and put a couple of drops of water in a dent on the top. Mix that in and continue with more drops until all of it is mixed and it looks like a peanut butter ball. This was then applied to the burned area. We wrapped it. She was instructed to keep it moist and to continue to apply the mixture until the area re-forms scabs. On the scabbed area, we would start that healing with the *Complete Tissue Formula* (Discussed earlier).

Little at a time these very deeply burned areas heal over and very little scar tissue resulted.

The Simplicity of Herbal Health

I had a family referred to me by some students. The parents called because their small son had fallen into a leaf pile that was burning and he had burns on his legs. The parents told me that their son was in the hospital and the doctors were debriding his legs daily while the parents held each other tightly as their son screamed. The son is screaming while on morphine. I told them that there is nothing that I can do to help them. If they try to take their son out of the hospital, child welfare will take custody away from the parents because they will be told that he would not be getting "proper care".

On to better things. Dr. Christopher suggested that making a fomentation of Slippery Elm would heal bedsores. He suggested applying it about ¾ of an inch thick, then keep it wet with hot towels. As it is absorbed, add more and it will go in and make new flesh.

Dr. Christopher said that it has been known to grow new hip joints and knees. When he said this, he also said that anyone with a bad hip or knees has no business running around anyway so they need to sit and read or something while this is growing back.

Here is a survival food. Herbs are food and George Washington's Army used this when they needed something to keep them alive according to The Little Herb Encyclopedia. Dr. Christopher mentioned that a gruel of Slippery Elm could be used to assist babies and the very elderly to gain or hold onto weight.

Because of its ability to disperse "inflammation and draw out impurities, Slippery Elm makes an excellent bolus (Suppository) to be used rectally to soothe any lower bowel irritation" according to Dr. Ritchason.

* * *

Dr. Christopher mentioned many times that the body could be fed through the skin. I put this to the test when my Mom had her stroke and couldn't swallow.

My sister's and I had her released from the hospital against the Doctor's advice. The Doctor kept telling us that without Mom's intravenous solution, she wouldn't last long. We did our best to agree but as soon as she was home with her caregiver, I went to work applying water poultices on both legs. (Remember in Chapter I, how much water the body needs?) Then we put herbal poultices on both arms. Next, we applied one of many oils to her torso. (We will be talking about the value of oil later in this Chapter.)

Now to help her learn to swallow, in the hospital they put a stainless steel rod in her mouth and pushed it into her throat to activate the "gag" reflex, we did it differently.

I pureed fresh peaches in the blender, adding just enough cooked grain (mostly rice) to thicken it. Then we would give her a drop from the end of a straw. (In Chapter I, we also mentioned that the mouth is the only place where we taste things.) We told her to suck on the straw if she wanted more of that taste. We made a lot of different tastes from all kinds of fruits. We even made a "malt" from pot roast with vegetables, Mom's favorite food.

She worked at getting these tastes as we continued to feed her body through the skin. The first week she was drinking only a couple of ounces orally a day. By the second week she was doing much better.

When we heard a gurgle, we told her to cough real hard and if she didn't, we would have to take her back to the hospital, we didn't need the complication of food in the lungs. She wasn't about to go back there so she followed instructions very well.

By the third week we were back to a spoon but she still liked her fruit "malts." At one time in this process, I was sure that she wasn't getting much food, then realized that a blender holds 18 to 20 ounces of whatever we were making. By then we had started finger foods and spoons, yet Mom was still drinking a couple of these "Malts" a day. So even without medical training we can use "natural" methods to help each other.

Making A Skin Salve

Let's find out how to make a skin **salve**: First we need to decide what we want it to do. Do we want it to handle rough skin? Or itching? Or something to pull toxins out?

We start out with some Extra Virgin Olive Oil. Olive oil has a long shelf life without going rancid like some oils do. In class I usually start out with 24 ounces of oil in a 2-quart saucepan. It is necessary to warm this oil but never let it get hot.

Next we combine the herbs that we wish to use with our heated oil. In this skin **salve** we are going to put 1 ounce of Comfrey leaves, 1 ounce of Plantain Leaves, and 1 ounce of Chickweed. After the herbs are stirred into the oil, we simmer this for 40 minutes to allow the constituents of the plants to be drawn into the oil.

When you make your skin **salve**, decide what you want in it or want it to do. In the summer one might use Citronella leaves (to keep the bugs away) along with Calendula (to soften the skin)

Now it is time to strain the oil off the herbal combination and return the infused oil into a clean saucepan. I originally used a sieve lined with a cloth but I would end up with burned fingers so I have changed my methods. I now spoon this oil-herb combination into a bulk tea press.

After pressing the infused oil has been returned to the cleaned saucepan and it is time to add bee's wax. There are many ways to measure the amount of wax needed. I have found that the easiest way for me is to put some wax in and allow it to melt. After it has melted, using a metal spoon, I dip a little out and dunk it in ice water. The wax hardens quickly and I know if my preparation is hard enough or if it is too hard. Then I either add more wax or more oil until it is the desired consistency.

Another way to check on the consistency is to put this spoon into the refrigerator for 2 minutes and then check for hardness. I am too impatient for this.

A third way is to measure one unit of wax to ten units of oil.

Using wide-mouth little jars, I pour the liquid into them and allow it to cool. As it cools, essential oils may be added. Some of my students like to add lavender oil to this skin cream. Then we label, always remember to label anything that you make.

The combination of herbs that we used for this **salve** would be a healing, drawing and anti-itch. When you decide to make your salve, you can use any other herbs in the manner that we just did.

One of the things that I like to do to quicken the process is to shave the wax so that it will melt faster. This is just a preference of mine.

When making suppositories (**Bolus**), we use this same method, but instead of using Olive Oil we melt Cocoa-butter. This will melt at body temperature and for a vaginal or anal suppository straining the herb/herbs out of the oil is not necessary. As it cools, use waxed paper to form it into a suppository shape. These can be put in the refrigerator or freezer until needed. After using them vaginally, a mild douche can be used to clean the area of herbal residue.

There are many other oils that can be used and experimented with. When using oil or even taking a gelcaps, always check to see that the oil is not rancid. With gelcaps we can poke one of them with a pin and squeeze some oil out so that you can smell it. Never put rancid oil into your body.

Do not use the product if you have overheated the oil and burned the herbs.

Organic oils are wonderful things. When the body is subjected to mineral oils, the nutritive value is drained off before the body assimilates them. Vegetable oils are accepted internally when taken in small quantities. There are exceptions to all the rules, the fact is that the brains needed large amounts of fats and oils with certain conditions.

Dr. Christopher also mentioned that, " if two-thirds of the skin is clogged, a person will die because there is not enough oxygen entering through the nose and lungs to meet the full body requirement." By clogging the skin with oily substances we are creating a problem that we sometimes use the oily substances to handle.

Olive Oil is a sweet nutritive, astringent and a laxative. It will help with abrasions, dry skin, even with high blood pressure.

* * *

It is time to tell you about an oil that has attracted my attention, Coconut oil.

My interest in this oil started with an e-mail from a former student. She wrote to tell me that she had lost a lot of weight. I congratulated her and asked her how she did it. She told me that she was frosting a bran muffin every morning with coconut oil and that was it. When I showed this to my husband, he wanted to know if that was all she was eating. So I asked. She then laid out the program. She did the frosted muffin one-hour after she got up and after that she ate whatever she wanted to. When she told me about her food intake, she also included a protest that I not evaluate her food, as my students are aware of my feeling and thoughts about food. She did mention that within the first few months, sugar or sweet things weren't tasty, and that soda tasted like battery acid. So some good was coming out of this.

My first thought was that this oil was lining the intestines and that the weight loss was from lack of nutrition. This started my search for answers.

I went to a local health food store and asked them about it. They were very excited about coconut oil and gave me a handout that had a list of the things Coconut oil would or could do. The list said that it could kill viruses that cause Mononucleosis, Hepatitis C, Measles, Herpes, and even AIDS. That is a big bill. But it also told me that it was antibacterial and that it killed fungi and yeast. It is supposed to aid digestion and provide a nutritional source for quick energy. The informational sheet also said that it protects against kidney disease and bladder infections. It is lower in calories than all other fats and here was the big one for me, it supports thyroid function. It went on and on about the benefits of this oil.

Next, I went into Dr. Duke's Database and didn't find anything there so I wrote to Dr. Duke. What I got back was amazing. He mentioned that he had written about coconut and its oils in a book called <u>CRC Handbook of Alternative Cash Crops</u>. He sent five pages of information about the constituents in Coconut oil. In his communication he wrote, "As you look at my database SD means seed, and the fatty acids listed for SD would be the components of the oil, which is highly regarded by some neomodern nutritionist, despised by soya oil enthusiasts." Apparently he feels that the Soya people put out the propaganda about coconut oil not being good for us...popcorn-wise?

* * *

Let's discuss fatty acids here because they are so helpful for the skin. One such plant is Purslane. Here is a weed that grows in any cultivated area and is loaded with Omega-3 fatty acids. We know that they inhibit cancers and are essential to every cell to make them function properly.

Purslane can be used in the same manner as aloe for burns or abrasions on the skin.

Mrs. Grieve mentioned that Purslane will provide substance for long journeys, "...that 2 or 3 ounces a day are quite sufficient for a man, even while under going great fatigue." This must be because it is so rich in vitamins and minerals.

This plant has been used for hundreds of years as food. Because of its succulent leaves and stems it has been pickled and even used to make soap.

According to Duke's Database, out of the almost 100 different constituents in this plant many of them were antiinflammatory and antibacterial, along with being antioxidant, and antiviral. Some even had sunscreen properties, while others were cancer preventive.

So here is another reason to eat weeds.

People with Vitiligo (White patches where the pigment is missing) can use this fatty acid or Flax Seeds or even Evening Primrose along with increasing the circulation internally and externally. This is basically from lack of nutrition to the skin. We need to feed our skin too.

Scar tissue can be handled many ways. Dr. Christopher suggests using a Comfrey paste, while Hanna suggests that can be handled with 5 tablespoons of good oil in 1 pint of cottage cheese. Mix and eat this for 3 days. She mentioned that anything could be added to make it taste good.

The Simplicity of Herbal Health

Hanna mentioned that Gold helps the body with collagen. As we wear gold against our skin, it is being absorbed in small amounts. There are some herbs that contain a trace amount of gold.

* * *

Another problem that people have with the skin is Rosacea. This is a ruddy complexion. The medical profession does not know what this is from and some of the things that they suggest tend to make it worse. The skin being the largest organ in the body takes a beating when the rest of the body isn't functioning. My first suggestion would be to start with Chapter 1 of this book and make sure that the toxins can get out. Then proceed to Chapter II, cleaning up the liver. When excessive chemicals are being processed, along with excessive hormones, and anything else that has been dumped into the body, it will react.

Many people think that the sun brings on a lot of this and it may be so if the body is already overloaded with photosensitive chemicals. Hanna suggested that being allergic to the sun could be a tuberculosis miasma. Hanna suggests that a Miasma is something attached to the DNA that was handed down "to the seventh generation."

David Slater of Boulder mentioned in his speech on Healers Who Share, that the greater majority of the population has inherited tags on the DNA from an ancestor who had tuberculosis. This "tag" as it were, might be interfering with the body's ability to deal with exposure to ultraviolet rays. Miasma is something that was inherited. It weakens the area in which it is attached but according to Hanna, most do not take the same form as the original problem.

In my family Tuberculosis miasma is prevalent and it takes the form of foot problems. It is easy to know which branch of the family tree it came from based on which cousins have foot problems. But this miasma could take the form of Scoliosis, Hammer toe, Bunions, Weak lungs or enlarged finger joints.

Hanna also mentions that Lupus responds to two of her vibrationals, *TB Residue* and *Thuja* but it takes up to three years to "interrupt this miasm."

* * *

Psoriasis can also be a problem. These are rough patches of skin. Again we start with the liver (Milk Thistle) and omega fatty acids are suggested. But most fats are to be avoided. Some of the herbs that are helpful are Licorice, Chamomile, along with Chickweed. My son found it helpful to use the sunshine to eliminate this problem. For him it was always worse in the winter. Hanna has a vibrational that can be used but it takes as long as 14 months to do this. Her vibrational is called *Syphonium*.

Acne is another skin problem that we bump into and Hanna's suggestion is to put a poultice of Comfrey on the right arm over night to help the body rid itself of acne. She also mentioned that with teenagers it stems from hormonal imbalance. We will be talking more about this later.

One of the other things that can happen to the skin has to do with a virus and they are called warts, we will also mention moles here. We talked about how my sister used Black Walnut Tincture in Chapter IV. Hanna mentioned that for warts and moles one could use the milk from the milkweed plants. She suggests putting the sap on the wart or mole, two times a day and says that they will turn black and fall off.

Hanna also mentioned in her lecture that staph is a decaying condition. It can be found in hospitals and doctor's offices. Children with this condition don't want to eat or be touched. The person with a staph condition is tired all the time. She created a vibrational for this called *Staff*. She also has a *Strep-Staph* combination in vibrational form.

My husband had a boil on his back and I suggested using a drawing salve. This is to draw it to a head and allow the matter inside to come out. Another person who had done this program had worked at it for a month, it finally opened and drained. When it was draining clear liquid it was time to heal it with a skin salve.

Hanna suggested putting sunflower petals in oil in the sun for 10 days and shake it daily. Then put it on the boils, two times a day and "tell them to go away."

Some of the drawing salves that are available or that you may wish to make contain Chickweed or Plantain. Dr. Christopher has a *Black Drawing Ointment* that contains Chaparral leaves, Comfrey root, Red Clover blossoms, Pine Tar, Mullein leaves, Beeswax, Lobelia, Goldenseal

The Simplicity of Herbal Health

root, Marshmallow root, Plantain leaves, Mutton tallow, Chickweed herb, and Poke root.

My favorite herb for drawing things out is Plantain. It grows everywhere and can be used to draw toxins out of the body when it is eaten. It can be crushed and added to a little oil then applied to a sting or bite and in this manner even be used to draw the toxin out of a nail hole on the bottom of the foot, eliminating lockjaw. In this same manner it will stop bleeding and pain. Internally it has been used to assist the healing of the lungs.

According to <u>The New Age Herbalist</u>, "Its silica and tannin content make it (Plantain) useful in treating varicose veins and hemorrhoids."

I was introduced to a woman that showed me her foot. It was beet-red and enlarged to the point of being hard. She had sores on the under side of the toes and a rather large one on her heel. She told me that they had been there a while. I was surprised that the enlargement and redness didn't go up the leg at all. I suggested using Plantain Salve on the sores. Then to get the blood moving, she was to put the foot in warm water for a while and then in cold water, back and forth at least once a day. I saw her a few months later and the foot was the normal size. She showed me the sores that looked more like scar tissue than sores. She mentioned that the Plantain salve had drawn out a lot of toxin. She had even showed the salve to her doctor because he had told her that they would never heal. When she used what he had given her, nothing happened so she was excited about the herbal stuff.

Mrs. Grieves talks about Plantain being used for Spider bites but I learned that spiders put an enzyme under the skin when they bite, unlike other bugs. This enzyme starts to break down the cell walls and then we get a red streak from the bite area up the body. Echinacea has been helpful for spider bites. Put a drop of Echinacea tincture directly on the bite and it will hold the integrity of the cells while it starts the healing.

The seeds of Plantain are called psyllium and are found in a lot of bulk laxatives.

A tea of Plantain was considered to be beneficial to the kidneys.

* * *

Hanna had a few other tidbits of information that I want to include here about the skin. One was the use of Bindweed. This is the weed that winds its way around all your plants and strangles them if you don't pull it out. Put it into a blender and a poultice is made from it for skin cancer. It will not cure skin cancer but will stop further growth until you have decided how you want to handle it. The other bit of information on this subject is that one can make a paste of baking soda and camphor to use on skin cancer.

* * *

As homework for this Chapter, I would like to suggest making a Witch Hazel Facial Toner, a decoction, if you will. I hope that you will want to try to make some of the herbal preparations that I have talked about in this text. This way you will know how to do it when you need them.

Witch Hazel makes a wonderful astringent wash for the face. The Witch Hazel that we buy bottled in stores is very drying to the skin as it is made with alcohol.

We use 1 tablespoon of dried Witch Hazel leaf or bark, and put it into 1 cup of distilled of water. After soaking it in this water for ½ hour, we simmer it for a short time. Strain, cool, bottle, and label it for later use. This preparation will stay fresh in the refrigerator for as long as 3 weeks. Normally a tea will only last a day or so but this one is stable longer because of the astringency of the herb. Use cotton balls to apply it to the face and feel the cells tighten.

Keep a record of how you do this so you can repeat or alter it, as you need to. Have fun and remember nature is wonderful.

The Bible talks about the fruit of the tree being used for food and the leaves for medicine.

Sexual Health

The first thing I would like to start with is Papilloma Virus. This is a virus, it is not cancer. Virus live inside of host cells and cause them to look strange so when you have your Pap smear what they are looking for is the "Flu" or virus in the cell.

I get rather excited about this subject because before I got into herbs, I was told that I had a class 4 Pap test. This is supposed to be serious. I was advised to have my organs removed. I really worried as anyone would, but I worked in the office of a medical clinic so I said that I wanted more tests. One can be done every 6 weeks. We sent them to various labs and they came back with different readings. We put some under other names and they came back different. I had biopsies done and sent in. The information was inconclusive. Finally I consented to having cone surgery. This is where they cut the cervix out in the form of a cone, freeze it and then slice it up into layers to recheck it. Remember they are still looking for a virus. Guess what? They didn't find anything after 8 months of doing all of this. I would never go through all this "hell" again now that I know what is available.

Hanna Kroeger treats this virus just like she treats the flu. Anybody, male or female, can get one of the 73 different Papilloma viruses. Hanna developed an herbal formula that she called *PAP*. It consists of Blue Flag Root, Blue Malva Flower, Blue Vervain, Papaya leaf, and Mullein leaf. But that isn't all. She has a *Papilloma* vibrational remedy that can be used in combination with the herbs.

Hanna says that this virus does not stay in one place. She says that it can go to any part of the body without one knowing that they have it. Some of the symptoms are: tiredness, genital warts, dysplasia, lack of concentration, forgetfulness, endometriosis, and of course an abnormal Pap smear.

This isn't just a female problem because it is directly linked to anal cancer and about half of the cases of penile cancer.

There are so many antivirus herbs that I could write a chapter on just them. Dr. Duke's database gave us some. Oregano has 22 antiviral properties in it, Tomato has 19, Common Thyme has 19, Green Tea has 18,

Rosemary has 18, Carrot has 16, Fennel has 16, Camomile has 16, Black Currant has 16. Even oranges and grapefruit have 15 different things in them that give them an antiviral property. And these aren't even the ones that I would choose.

Papilloma is not something to be afraid of, we just need to know that it is there and then we handle it. Our bodies are self-healing. (I heard that from a phone call that I just took) There is only one dis-ease and that is constipation or congestion. If we get the toxins out and the nutrition in, we can heal.

* * *

David Christopher, the Director of the School of Natural Healing in Springville, Utah and I agree on a lot having to do with women's health. David asked the question, "Why do women allow the medical profession to do all the things to them that they do?" He was referring to Hysterectomies, C-sections, Breasts taken off, and the high volume of drugs that are prescribed.

Hanna Kroeger says that most female problems are because we are out of balance. She thinks that all of the electrical things in our lives, Computers, Stoves, TV, Refrigerators, Washing machines, Fax machines, Zerox machines, Printers, Cell phones, and what have you are hard on women. Women are magnetic and Men are electronic so men don't have a problem with all of the electronic equipment that is throwing women out of balance. She has an herbal product called *Female Balance* that contains Black Cohosh, Anise Seeds, Yellow Dock, and Ginger Root.

David talked about Hysterectomies being done for excessive bleeding. This is usually caused by an imbalance of hormones. Doctor Christopher suggested Sarsaparilla Tea every half-hour. (We are not talking about a cancerous condition here.) It could even be related to a hypo or hyper thyroid. We know what to do for the thyroid. (Check Chapter II) Polyps or endometriosis can cause heavy bleeding. Maybe it is being caused by a miscarriage or an IUD or even things that have gotten lost in there (it does happen).

Hanna felt that there might be bacteria involved with heavy bleeding. She also suggested brushing five times down both sides of the body to balance the auric energy.

The Simplicity of Herbal Health

Dr. Christopher suggested stopping the use of animal products as this builds up an acid condition in the body. He thought that using wheat germ oil, flax seed oil or eating purslane might be helpful. With heavy bleeding there is a low iron and vitamin A deficiency. They only contribute to the heavy bleeding. We need to build up the blood so that it will hold the iron. Wheat grass, well, all green things will help build our blood supply. There is only one chemical difference between our blood and that of plants. Shredded wheat is high in iron but soaked whole wheat is more iron friendly. Hydrochloric acid is needed to use the available iron. With antacids there is no acid in the body that is needed for the utilization of minerals. Dr. Christopher suggested some herbs that might be helpful with heavy bleeding. They are: Chickweed, Kelp, Dandelion, Sunflower seeds, Beet juice, even raisins. He suggests that we stop drinking milk or eating eggs, as these will block the body's ability to use iron. Coffee and Tea block this ability to use iron. Calcium supplements do the same thing, as they are all alkaline.

For Fibroid Tumors, Hanna suggested that 10 days before the onset of a period, put molasses in a #2 jell cap and insert it in the vagina each night. Rinse it out with chamomile tea in the morning. Do this until the period starts and the fibroids will come out with the menses. I would probably do this in conjunction with False Unicorn Capsules or tincture.

When the menstrual cycle has stopped, it is usually from malnutrition or congestion or hormonal. Cleansing and feeding the body will correct it. Contrary to the advertising that you see on TV, you can not run a marathon on Pepsi. If you are feeding the body, you can exercise all you want and there will be no problem.

Did you know that plant hormones (phytosterols) make hormones in our bodies? We need the nourishment that plants give to us. Our pets are having the same problems that we are. They aren't getting nutrition for their bodies either. I have many friends who are making their own pet food this reason. For recipes check in <u>The New Natural Cat</u> by Anitra Frazier, <u>Natural Pet Cures</u> by Dr. John Heinerman, or <u>The Natural Remedy Book For Dogs And Cats</u> by Diane Stein.

Endomitosis is when uterus cells are growing in the abdominal cavity. This is not normal. Normally when a cell is working in the wrong place, the body recognizes it and destroys that cell. So how did we get to this? David

Christopher wants to blame birth control pills that are building up estrogen in the body, allowing these cells to function in the wrong place. I think that they are partly to blame but the chemicals in plastic are loaded with estrogenic properties, we are feminizing this planet. David also thought tampons might just be blocking the normal discharge pattern. One of the herbs that he suggests is a lot of Red Raspberry leaf tea and doing a full cleanse.

Hanna treats Endomitosis like Candida, no carbohydrates, not even bananas.

PMS – see Chapter II

Water retention was covered in at the beginning of this Chapter with kidneys.

Menopause is interesting and I can't believe how many people have a problem with this. For centuries, women went through menopause without the help of a doctor. Here, I agree with David when he says that the problem is caused by our life style. We are eating foods that have no value. Penny Kelly talked about that in Chapter I. We aren't getting the needed minerals, vitamins and phyto-chemicals that are in wholesome foods. Wild plants have what we need. They aren't messed up from our farming processes. There aren't Black Cohosh farms. My favorite herb is Sarsaparilla because it doesn't build estrogen, it doesn't build progesterone, it doesn't build testosterone but gives the body the building blocks to make whichever one of these three that is needed.

Hanna suggested Licorice root and Wild Cherry bark as two herbs that would be helpful with menopause. For hot flashes, her suggestion was to hold the back of the left knee for a few minutes. (This has never worked for me, but then I have never had a major problem.)

Hanna mentioned that Estrogen pills are cancer forming. They are just discovering what Hanna talked about 10 to 15 years ago. The chemical companies are now suggesting a "Viagra" for women. These chemicals are messing us up. This brings us back to David Christopher's original question, "Why do women allow this?"

Ovarian cysts can be a problem for a lot of women. Kroeger Herb has an herbal tea formula called *FML* made up of Calendula and Yarrow

The Simplicity of Herbal Health

flowers along with Nettle leaves. Hanna suggested 4 cups of this a day for 21 days to handle this problem. For lumps on the ovaries she suggests making a tea of two parts Calendula, one part plantain, one part yarrow. She suggests drinking a quart daily for 4 weeks.

Herbs are foods. Unless you are working on a specific problem, vary what you take. Never take the same thing all the time.

A nurse called me to ask for a list of herbs that were estrogenic. The list was: Black Cohosh, Dong Quai, Eucalyptus, Fennel Oil, Blue Cohosh, Burdock Rt., Hops, Ginseng, Red Clover, Licorice, Red Raspberry, Sage and Chaste berry. But we don't really need more estrogen, we need a balance. Chaste Berry, Wild Yam Root and Sarsaparilla will give us the phytosterols to make whatever we need from progesterone to testosterone. Men need these as much as we do because of our depleted foods. Saw Palmetto is great for both sexes. Dandelion Root cooked is great for the prostate.

Osteoporosis! Now there is a word that is scaring everyone these days. Why do you think that is? Because we are losing calcium and we keep packing it in. David Christopher suggests that we are losing it because of our high protein diet. He thinks that the Basic 4 Food Groups that are taught in our school systems is creating this problem because it recommends a high protein diet. When protein goes up, calcium goes down.

Teenagers are eating the nutritionally deficient foods that are creating the discontent, and young girls are starting periods as early as 9 year old and some earlier. With a cup of Red Raspberry leaf tea, this would balance out.

Soda water or pop, will get rid of calcium in the body. Sugar does it too because the body needs calcium 2/1 with phosphorus. Sugar gets rid of half of the phosphorus in the body. There is no calcium in sugar but David suggested that if you take 4 teaspoons of sugar, the blood calcium would go up. The body needs calcium so it sends chemicals out to dissolve calcium from the bones. Sugar is the best way to cause "potato chip" bones.

Most health magazines talk about fat and salt as a major health problem. They even tell you that peanuts and avocados are bad due to

Phyllis Heitkamp Master Herbalist

their high fat content but have no problem with all the sugar that we are consuming. Sugar is probably the number 1 killer in America today.

There are a lot of sweeteners like Sucanut or Stevia out there for us to use, but for the most part we need to use other flavors on a daily basis. There is sour, pungent and bitter, and what do we do with sour? We make it sweet and sour.

Milk is a high protein and alkaline. We need acid to utilize calcium so with lots of milk, we are really losing calcium.

Did you know that we get about three times the calcium than Asians do and we have twice the bone breakage? It is our life style. We have bone spurs and arthritis and are breaking bones.

Let's go out to dinner here, what is on the menu? Will you be having our chicken breast or our sirloin steak tonight? Thank you, and that is a good choice. What type of potato do you want? We have baked, French fries, or cottage fries. Very good. For your vegetable, your choices are our carrot and pea combination or our roasted corn on the cob? Very good, let's see if I have your order? You want half of the plate covered with our choice sirloin steak (High protein and fat), and you have decided on the baked potato (a cup of sugar in a casing...potato starch breaks down into a simple carbohydrate in a very short time), along with the two tablespoons of over cooked carrots and peas. Or Maybe you have chosen the half plate of chicken (Same deal), the fried potatoes (Same deal) and the corn (another simple carbohydrate that will be a sugar before you leave the table.) And we are a country that eats out.

We need trace minerals in our diets. Vitamin companies will acknowledge that we need magnesium and maybe one or two other thing like folic acid with our calcium but that isn't all we need. We need Silica. Did you know that people with high silica in the blood would have their bones heal faster? Silica is in whole grains but not in pasta, not in sugar, not in processed foods. It is in Dulse and Horsetail grass. Dr. Christopher's formula called *Calcium Assimilation Formula* is high in silica. Dr. Christopher told us that a person could reverse osteoporosis by using this formula along with Apple Cider Vinegar and his *Vitalerbs*, a complete herbal vitamin formula. If I were doing it, I would recommend adding the *Complete Tissue Formula* to this. My collarbone was healed quickly using this method.

The Simplicity of Herbal Health

* * *

Yeast is an interesting problem. Candida Albicans is necessary to break down sugar and alcohol in the body. It has a purpose. One way to get an over growth of it is to take an antibiotic. Another way is to use Colloidal Silver. Colloidal Silver kills the flora as sure as an antibiotic because silver is an antibiotic.

When we want to get rid of Candida, we need to stop eating what feeds it, sugar and alcohol. All of the sweets do this, honey, maple syrup.

* * *

Here is the Healer Who Share's Candida program.

"Things that are OK to eat:
Meats, Poultry, Fish
Eggs
Vegetables of most kinds except corn
Tomatoes and tomato sauce
Avocados
Plain Yogurt
Rice –Rice cakes, Rice syrup, Rice flour, Rice pasta, Rice milk and cheese
Tahini (Crushed sesame seed, like peanut butter)
Salads with lemon and olive oil dressing
Herbal and Black tea
Water
Butter and spices
Terra Chips (Excluding orange colored potato chips)

Omit from the diet
Fruits and fruit juices, Sugars, Fructose, Artificial sweeteners, Chocolates
Honey, Molasses, Dextrose, Sucrose or any "ose" ingredient.
Potatoes, Pasta Tortillas, Beans
Corn, Popcorn, Corn flakes or Corn flour
Bread, Wheat, Cereals of Wheat or Oats
Yeast containing products including yeast based vitamins, canned soups

Any form of bread with yeast
Alcohol, Beer, Wine, Sodas
Vinegar, Sauerkraut, fermented products
Mushroom and other fungi
Coffee in limited amount
Dairy products, Milk, Cheese
Soy products
Nuts and Nutbutters

The first three days can be a bumpy ride. Yeast detoxification creates an effect on the body and at first your energy can go down, you may feel low-grade flu symptoms or headaches. You may experience mild diarrhea or constipation. These symptoms should be low-grade and not take you out of your daily routine.

You should expect to feel extra tired and give yourself extra rest during this time. Be sure to drink extra amounts of water to speed up your detoxification. After the three-day period, your energy will gradually come up over a ten-day period. About the third week, your body will adjust to your new diet and you will begin to feel better and better.

About cheating: if you cheat on the diet, small buds of yeast will blossom. Your energy will go down following "a cheat", as the body has to detoxify the budded yeast. Try to hold firm the first three months.

If you carry excess weight, this diet may shed 15 to 20 pounds per month.

After completing three months of strictly adhering to the diet you may begin experimenting by bringing in the following foods: nuts, nut butters, quince and soy products. Stay off the balance of the forbidden foods for the entire six months."

The previous information came from the Healers Who Share's information. For more information about them check: healerswhoshare.com web page

* * *

When candida takes over, it drills holes in the intestine and from there it mimics every disease. It can take 6 weeks to cure, 6 months and if not

The Simplicity of Herbal Health

done well it can take 6 years. Herbs that are helpful are: Pau du Arco, Black Walnut and Garlic.

One of the best ways to fill the intestinal tract with new flora is with Rejuvelac. This is made by taking a glass and filling it one-fourth full of a whole grain, Wheat berries, Oat Grouts, any whole grain. Then fill the glass to the top with water, cover and allow this to set. After 24 hours it will start to bubble and smell strange. The water is then drunk. (Maybe with your nose being held?) This fermented water contains the entire flora that is needed to regain the balance in the intestinal tract once again.

Fermented products like sauerkraut have friendly flora but cooked foods don't, and you won't find them on food that has been sprayed with chemicals to keep the produce from sprouting.

* * *

So how can we help ourselves during Menopause? Dr. Christopher has an herbal product called *Hormonal Changease*. It contains: Black Cohosh, Sarsaparilla, American Ginseng, Licorice, False Unicorn, Blessed Thistle, and Squaw Vine. He also has a product called *Female Reproductive Formula* and it contains: Goldenseal, Blessed Thistle, Cayenne, Cramp Bark, False Unicorn Root, Ginger, Red Raspberry leaves, Squaw Vine, and Uva Ursi leaves. These plants give the body the building blocks that we are not getting in our foods.

Both of the products mentioned above have False Unicorn in them, so let me tell you a little about False Unicorn. Dr. Christopher told us that False Unicorn would clean up and repair the reproductive organs. After he told us about it a couple of my friends wanted to have a baby and were not able to conceive, I suggested that both the husband and the wife take False Unicorn capsules. There is a baby girl on this planet called Lee that is a False Unicorn baby. Another couple named their False Unicorn baby, Serena.

Another lady told me that she found out that the mucus in her body was killing her husband's sperm. I suggested that she eat only alkaline foods for three days and then only acid foods. I gave her a list of what was what. She told me that it was very hard to eat the alkaline foods but she did it. When she went back to her gynecologist for some tests, she was told that the balance in the mucus was the best it could be. She has since had a baby boy.

* * *

Another subject that would be good to address here is incontinence. Hanna suggested that it could be a kidney infection or that it could come from stress. She felt that any household that had a female in it should have a package of whole cranberries in the freezer. The cranberry juice that you get in the store is mostly water but when you cook your own cranberries and get the juice from them, you have a powerful helper. Cranberries do not kill the bacteria but make the walls of the bladder slick so nothing can stick to it. This flushes the bacteria out quickly.

Dr. Christopher created a product called *Bladder Formula* and it contains: Parsley Root, Juniper Berries, Marshmallow Root, White Pond Lily, Gravel Root, Uva Ursa Leaves, Lobelia Herb, Ginger Root and Black Cohosh Root. The secret ingredient is the White Pond Lily. He even put this in a formula for bed wetters. (check Kidneys, earlier in this chapter.)

Dr. Christopher mentioned that by drinking Blessed Thistle tea, one could nurse a child "even if you have never been with a man." He talked about men nursing babies in some South American tribes while the women worked. It will enhance milk production when nursing twins.

Dill weed tea will promote milk production if it has slowed down or stopped. Hanna said that instead of milk: make a formula of one half oat milk and one half whole milk. No honey or bananas for babies until they are at least 4 months old.

Hanna suggested a warm corn syrup douche before intercourse if you want a baby and cold douche after intercourse if you don't want a baby. She also suggested 3 tansy leaves boiled in a quart of water. Drink 3 cups a day for 3 days before your period as a female expectorant (Birth control.)

A lot of women have problems after childbirth because they return to work too early.

Hanna suggested pushing the insides of the knees for a tubular pregnancy.

The Simplicity of Herbal Health

* * *

I have one more thing that I would like to add here and that has to do with Mammograms. Do you think that they will find either a virus (Papilloma) or excessive hormones in an X-ray. There is something called a thermogram that works on temperature. I would do a thermogram but I do not support mammograms because I do not want radiation near my fatty tissue.

This is a planet of choice and we are all free to choose what we want done with our bodies. Choose wisely.

Chapter V - Resources

Christopher, David, MH, *Class lecture Notes,* 1996, www.snh.cc

Christopher, John R., Dr., *School Of Natural Healing,* Christopher Publications, Springville, UT, 1996, 724 pg. 1-800-372-8255

Duke, James A., Ph.D., *Duke's Phytochemical and Ethnobotanical Database,* 2003

Duke, J.A. and DuCellier, J.L., *CRC Handbook of Alternative Cash Crops,* CRC Press. Boca Raton. FL. 536 pg.

Foster, Steven, *Herbal Renaissance,* Gibb Smith, Layton, UT, 1957, 234 pg.

Grieves, Mrs., *A Modern Herbal,* Dover Publications, Inc., NY, 1971, 902 pg.

Kroeger, Hanna, Rev., *God Helps Those Who Help Themselves,* 1984, 269 pg.

Kroeger, Hanna, Rev., *Heal Your Life with Home Remedies and Herbs,* Hay House, Inc., Carlsbad, CA., 1998, 296 pg.

Mabey, Richard, Editor, *The New Age Herbalist,* Simon and Schuster Inc. NY., 1988, 288 pg.

Ritchason, Jack, ND, *The Little Herb Encyclopedia,* Woodland Health Books, Pleasant Grove, Utah, 1995, 402 pg.

Shook, Edward E., Dr., *Advanced Treatise in Herbology,* Trinity Center Press, Beaumont, CA., 1978, 359 pg.

Strehlow, Wighard, Dr., Hertzka, Gottfried, MD, *Hildegard of Bingen's Medicine,* Bear and Company, Santa Fe, NM, 1988, 161 pg.

Tyler, Varro, E., PhD.,*Herbs of Choice,* Pharmaceutical Products Press, N.Y, 1994, 209 pg.

Chapter VI
Tea Time

Before beginning this chapter, make a tea out of the herb of your choice. You have read about a lot of different herbs and it is time to decide which one you would like to try this time.

In only one of my many classes did a student ask me if I had milk or sugar for the tea that I served. I had to explain that we don't "do" milk and sugar. I serve tea so that my students can benefit from the healing effects of that tea and learn about the taste of each plant. According to Mrs. Grieve, before the English imported Green and Black tea, they didn't use milk or sugar either. Green and Black tea contain caffeine and true herbalists do not use caffeine substances. That is not to say that a Green Tea isn't good for you, as everyone knows it has some healing properties. The fermented leaves of Black Tea have always been too acidic for me to handle. A lot of people think of Green and Black tea as an herbal tea and in a way they are but, not to a true herbalist.

I hope that you have sampled enough different herbal teas while reading this book to have found a couple of favorites.

One exciting thing is to vary what you drink. As with everything else, we should vary what we eat and drink. I do this with herbs all the time because each one gives my body different things. Today I might have Nettle tea and tomorrow I might decide to have Lemon Grass or Chamomile.

Herbs are foods and just as we wouldn't eat the same thing day after day, we would not drink the same tea day after day.

I hope today's tea is enjoyable, whether it is a hot tea or an iced tea or a sun tea. Enjoy and allow all the benefits of your drink to add to the health of your body.

The Pancreas

The first subjects of this chapter have to do with the pancreas and diabetes.

David Christopher taught us about the five different kinds of diabetes. Most of us only know about one kind so I will try to tell you what David said.

He said that the five different kinds are Insipidus, Bronze, Gestational, Type 1 – Juvenile on-set and type 2 Non-insulin.

When he talked about Insipidus, he mentioned that this was a pituitary problem. The pituitary is a gland in the head. Remember in Chapter II, when we talked about how to heal glands? We mentioned that Mullein leaves heal glands. O-kay, so we have a gland in the head that needs to be healed. Let's make a formula for this. First we would start with the glandular healer, Mullein. Then let's add some herbs that go specifically to the brain…how about Gotu Kola or one of the other herbs that was mentioned in Chapter III, and let's add Alfalfa (found in Chapter IV) to send a lot of nourishment to that area. Remember that this healing can take 1 week or 1 year, depending on how we treat this body.

* * *

The next kind that he talked about was Bronze. This is where the blood can't hold iron. The blood is weak and we need to build it where it can hold iron. In an earlier Chapter we talked about the fact that plant blood is very closely related to human blood. There is just one thing that is different, so to build our blood, we would want a lot of plant blood as in chlorophyll. This could be from Alfalfa, Chlorella, Spirulina or any of the juices of green plants. Then we might want to add one of the blood cleansers that we talked about in Chapter II (Red Clover, Burdock or Chaparral.) And if you remember, when we talked about sugars we talked about Molasses as high in almost everything that the blood needs to get balanced and in this case, Iron. When the blood is built up a little, one of the docks might be nice as Yellow Dock is high in useable iron.

* * *

The Simplicity of Herbal Health

The third kind of diabetes that we want to discuss here is Gestational. This is a lifestyle problem. It can be temporary or permanent. It starts in the last half of pregnancy and it is all due to diet. It can be corrected with a correct diet and here we are talking about the five things that Dr. Christopher always talked about, Fruits, Vegetables, Whole Grains, Nuts and Seeds. We can't make a baby eating like a teenage girl. Hamburgers and coke are not suitable to build a second body, let alone keep the original body healthy.

* * *

This brings us to Adult on-set Diabetes, with 12 to 14 million people have this in the United States according to the Diabetic Statistics of 2000. It is costing us 137.7 billion dollars to take care of this problem.

Fact: Americans have one-fifth the chromium in their bodies that Asians have. This happens because we lose 300% of our Chromium when we eat refined carbohydrates. Chromium controls the sugar level in our blood.

Juniper berries are high in Chromium, as is Spirulina.

Spirulina (Algae pratensis) is a blue-green algae. Dr. Ritchason tells us that it "is a one-celled form of algae that multiplies in warm, alkaline freshwater bodies. Germs and scum, are associated with microorganisms of disease. Spirulina grows in this type of surrounding but it is, in fact, one of the cleanest, most naturally sterile foods found in nature. The ability of Spirulina to grow in hot and alkaline environments ensures its hygienic status. As no other organisms can survive to pollute the waters in which this algae grows." He goes on to tell us that it is "the highest source in the world of Beta carotene, Vitamin B-12 and gamma liolenic acid. Spirulina contains most of the known amino acids. It contains all nine essential amino acids that the body must derive from food. It contains 250% more Vitamin B-12 than liver and four times the protein of beef. The proteins of Spirulina are 80 –85% assimilated as compared to 20% for beef."

Dr. Ritchason mentions that Spirulina contains 26 times the calcium of milk and lots of phosphorus and niacin. It can be stored for many years and still contain a high percentage of nutrients. The down side is that it lacks carbohydrates.

It satisfies hunger and balances blood sugar levels. It supplies nutrition for the brain and is one of the best blood, cell and tissue builders.

Dr. Duke's database tells us that this one-celled plant has 181 active properties. Here is a secret weapon for a lot of health problems and Diabetes is one of them. He mentions that it contains three properties that are "antidiabetic".

Other herbs that are high in Chromium are Nettle, as is Stevia, Barley Grass, Burdock, Bee Pollen and there are many more.

The body needs glucose as fuel to keep it running and the liver stores glucose and sends it out as the body needs it. The body needs 65 to 80 mg per milliliter of blood.

In a healthy body, the cells can't accept glucose unless there is insulin present. The pancreas makes the insulin and sends it out when there is glucose in the body. Sometimes it gets fooled into thinking that there is glucose out there when it is just sugar. The body can't use the sugar so when the insulin is released, the liver thinks that some glucose is needed and the body is first overloaded with insulin and then after it has washed out (along with the sugar), the body is overloaded with glucose. This goes back and forth so many times that the body doesn't know what is happening.

David Christopher feels that because we have been doing this to the body for years and years... (Most Diabetics become diabetic in their middle to late years) that the body is just very confused. Most adult-on-set diabetics have enough insulin but the body isn't responding because it has spent years in confusion.

One of the things that I have found is that most people do not know the difference between carbohydrates and <u>simple carbohydrates</u>. This is the contention that I have with the Atkin's diet. People come to me and tell me that they can't eat carbs. What they really mean is that they can't eat simple carbohydrates. These are foods that break down into sugar before they are done chewing them. I agree that corn and potatoes are what they can't have but most people think of all vegetables as carbs.

The biggest problems that vegetarians have is that they eat all these simple carbs. They eat a lot of pastas and breads thinking that these are

The Simplicity of Herbal Health

not carbs but grains. They are not grains. They are dead foods with very little value. Once you have squashed the grain, you have oxidized it and killed anything of value in it. Then they break down into sugars very quickly. Even school systems promote them as the grain part of the food pyramid. Pizza is not a complete food. It has a few vegetables ...maybe... on a lot of simple carbs. But then the argument is that it has cheese as a protein. It is a protein that unless one is drinking a lot of water, will slow the system down, making it sluggish.

"So what can I eat?" is the cry that I get from new diabetics. I finally made a list for them of Complex Carbohydrates (the good carbs) and it is as follows: Artichokes, Asparagus, Avocado, Beans, Beet Tops, Beets, Bok Choy, Broccoli, Brussels Sprouts, Cabbage, Carrots, Cauliflower, Celery, Chard, Chickpeas, Cress, Cucumbers, Dandelion roots, Egg Plant, Ginger Root, Green Beans, Green Peas, Green Pepper, Horseradish, Kale, Kohlrabi, Kraut, Leeks, Lettuce, Lima Beans, Mushrooms, Mustard Greens, Okra, Olives, Onions, Parsnips, Peppermint, Pumpkins, Radishes, Rutabaga, Scallions, Snow Peas, Spinach, Squash, Swiss Chard, Tomatoes, Turnips, Watercress, Wild Rice, Zucchini, and all Grains – whole and soaked, All Herbs, and all of the Nuts and Seeds.

On the <u>not to eat</u> list are Potatoes and Corn. David Christopher called a baked potato, "a cup of sugar in a casing."

On the "yes" list there are two things that are wonderful, Kohlrabi and Dandelion. They contain a property called inulin and can be assimilated by the body without the use of insulin. There is a third member of this family and it is Chicory Rt. Both Dandelion root and Chicory root are bitter when eaten as opposed to Kohlrabi, which is sweet. In order for the inulin to work, these plants must be eaten raw, when cooked or roasted the inulin is destroyed.

Why would one roast these roots? Chicory has been used as a substitute coffee for many years. When the dried root is roasted and ground up, it has a coffee like flavor. One can rinse the roots and leaves to purge some of the bitter out. The leaves are very high in Vitamin A, Calcium and Potassium and have enough of things like Iron, Vitamins C and B along with Phosphorus and many more properties that most plants need to stay healthy.

My granddaughter, Susan and I used to have a song that we sang about Chicory. As we drove, the first one to spot the bright blue flowers along the side of the road had to sing the "Chicory chic, chala chala, Checkermorony; in a bananaca. Ballaca, wallaca, can't you see, Chicory chic is me." It was silly but as she got older she remembered that there was something special about the little blue flower by the side of the road.

One of the interesting things about Chicory is that after it has been roasted other things develop in its roots, according to Steven Foster. "When Chicory is roasted, numerous flavoring components develop in the root, including maltol, a natural taste modifier which intensifies the flavor of sugar." Maltol is the ingredient that is found at the health food store in a lot of "sugarless" candies because it is not supposed to be absorbed by the body in the same manner as sugar.

Some of the things that Chicory is used for (other than a coffee substitute) are: for stomach problems, as an overall tonic, as a diuretic, a laxative and it has sedative qualities. It is anti-inflammatory but studies show that it will depress the heart rate and relax the heartbeat a bit.

* * *

In the chapter on sugar, I showed you a letter that I got from the ADA (American Diabetes Association) regarding sugars so I am not going to repeat it here but I do hope that any diabetic reading this book will be as anti-aspartame as I am. Many people have spoken out on this from Dr. H. J Roberts, Author of <u>Aspartame, Is it Safe</u>, <u>Sweetner Dearest, Is Aspartame Safe? A Medical, Public Health Legal Overview on Tape.</u> To Mary Nash Stoddard's, <u>The Deadly Deception.</u> And Barbara Alexander Mullarkey's, <u>Bittersweet Aspartame: A Diet Delusion.</u>

Artificial sweeteners trick the body and because there is no glucose, the body craves simple carbohydrates and gains weight. Even the fructose that is on the market is made with hydrochloric acid from corn syrup.

There are so many other things that can be used by diabetics to sweeten their foods such as Stevia. I grow Stevia in my house and for dessert, I pull two leaves from the plant, giving one to my husband and having one myself. Chewing on this leaf satisfies all the sweet at the end of a meal.

The Simplicity of Herbal Health

This plant tends to get lanky and a grower told me to "top" it and let it fill out. I did and I dried the leaves that came off. I now have a small container of Stevia leaves that my students sample. First I give them a little spoonful of processed liquid Stevia. Then I give them the real thing. They can really tell the difference between the fresh and the processed. It is all about wholesome not part-some, where the whole leaf versus leaves that have been processed with other things added.

We talk about ways to use Stevia. A little infusion can be made with the leaves and this infusion can be used to sweeten something, like a grapefruit. I tell them about coring apples and putting raisins in the middle along with some crumpled Stevia leaves and some cinnamon. We can learn to eat without sugar or Aspartame.

What I have seen is that diabetics "lean" on their insulin shots or pills. Two diabetics that I know still eat candy and cookies to the extreme. They just take their blood test and if the blood sugar is too high, they take more insulin or get it sooner than they would have if their blood sugar was lower. They have not learned how to eat. The American Diabetic Association has not helped any of the Nation's Diabetics. As you can see, I do not support this organization. I will when they can think for themselves and not follow the "guide lines" mapped out for them by the American Medical Association or the Food and Drug Association.

O-kay, so what can a diabetic do? Start by changing their environment. Clean up the body starting with Chapter I of this book and by using herbs. I talked about Juniper in an earlier Chapter so I will just mention that studies done in Spain show that Juniper berries reduce blood sugar and mortality in Diabetics. I want to mention Dr. Christopher's *Pancreas Formula* that contains: Goldenseal Root, Uva Ursi Leaves, Cayenne Pepper, Cedar Berries (Juniper Monosperma), Licorice Root, Mullein Leaves.

He felt that this formula would aid in the transfer mechanism and up-take of insulin.

Other herbs that are helpful in regulating blood sugar are; Ginseng, Bilberry, and Black Berry. Some that reduce the blood sugar are Aloe, Apple pectin, Celery seeds, Coriander, Black Cohosh, Garlic and Onions, Marshmallow Root, and Raspberry.

Dr. Christopher mentioned that one-half teaspoon of ground nutmeg in warm water would "jump start" the Pancreas.

Fenugreek was studied in India and it was found to be able to cut the blood sugar 54%. So when my sister Betty's blood sugar shot up while we were on a trip, we visited a health food store and bought some Fenugreek seeds. She carried these with her to chew on.

I want to tell you more about Fenugreek as explained by Dr. Ritchason. He tells us that Fenugreek was used by Hypocrites and considers it one of the "oldest known medicinal herbs." I can understand why because it does so many wonderful things. It is an "Alternative (produces a favorable change in the body or its metabolism), Aphrodisiac (increase sexual sensitivity), Aromatic (having a sweet fragrance), Astringent (agent that binds tissue), Carminative (reduces flatulence), Demulcent (a soothing agent), Emollient (a softening agent), Expectorant (expels secretions), Galactagogue (lactation-promoting agent), Hormonal (contains properties that create hormones), Laxative (bulk), Mucilant (loosens mucus), Nutritive (nourish body tissue), Parasiticide (destroys parasites), Stimulant (increases activity), Stomachic (stimulates the stomach's action), and Tonic (agent increasing strength and tone)." All of this from some little seeds!

Some of the other things that Dr. Ritchason came up with for Fenugreek are that it "has been used to help prevent pregnancies due to its spermicidal factors." And because of all the great properties in Fenugreek it is used for abscesses, allergies, anemia, asthma, blood poisonings, boils, bronchitis, lymph cancers, cholesterol...this is interesting because it is high in Lecithin, which "helps to dissolve cholesterol and fatty substances." There are so many more things that these little seeds can do so I will just quote Dr. Ritchason again with, "some have used Fenugreek with lemon juice and honey to soothe and nourish the body and to reduce fevers."

I think all of these are reason enough to plant a seed and have some on hand.

* * *

With **Low Blood Sugar**, we have a liver problem. The suggested solution is to clean the liver, as in Chapter II, along with using Dr. Christopher, *Pancreas Formula*. Then add another formula called the *Adrenal Formula*

The Simplicity of Herbal Health

that contains Mullein leaves, Licorice root, Lobelia, Ginseng, Gotu kola, Hawthorn Berries, Cayenne, and Ginger root.

Hanna Kroeger suggested that with low blood sugar, one might find parasites in the pancreas.

With **High blood Sugar**, we need to clean up the bowels, the liver, the blood, the pancreas and the adrenals. Dr. Christopher suggests his formulas that do just this...*Lower Bowel Formula, Liver and Gall Bladder Formula, Blood Stream Formula, Pancreas Formula,* and *Adrenal Formula*.

In addition to doing the formulas, it is imperative that we change our eating habits and get back to basics. The five foods that Dr. Christopher calls the "Mucusless Diet". Fruits, Vegetables, Whole grains, Nuts and Seeds will feed the body and keep it healthy. As the body is cleaned, less and less of the medication will be needed.

* * *

Let's talk about Juvenile Diabetes because more and more children are getting this disease. According to David Christopher, the medical profession believes that this comes from a viral infection but David doesn't believe that this is so.

He says what is happening is that the Beta cells are destroyed by the immune system. The immune system only destroys errant cells so why then is it doing this to cells that are supposed to be in the body? Did you know that Juvenile Diabetes is only diagnosed when 80% of the beta cells are destroyed?

Why would the immune system think that the beta cells are foreign to the body? David's theory is that perhaps foreign matter is combining with the beta cells and multiplying. The immune system recognizes the fact that these cells are self/not-self so it destroys them to be safe.

If foreign proteins have combined with these cells, they would have to be the exact weight and mirror the proteins that the beta cells need.

That sounds strange because protein does not go into the body as protein but rather is changed to Amino Acids and these are used by the body. So how would a foreign protein get into the body? In Chapter I, we talked about having a skin barrier inside and outside of the body to keep "foreign" things out, so how is this possible?

It could happen if something "foreign" is placed under the skin either by accident or by intention. Why would anyone intentionally put something under the skin? I really don't know, but a lot of people think it is the right thing to do and they call them vaccines.

Most of us who have gotten into natural health have had a turning point, a major health problem that the medical profession could not help us with. Hanna Kroeger's turning point was her small daughter. She had four children when she came to America and it was the last one that pushed her into what she did with the rest of her life.

She was told that her daughter needed to have vaccines in order to attend school in the United States. Hanna wanted to obey the rules so she had her youngest daughter vaccinated and she almost lost her. She promised God that if he would let her daughter live, she would spend the rest of her life helping people. The daughter lived, but is a 40-year-old person, who is still working at a 12-year-old level.

In the Milwaukee Journal-Sentinel, April of 2001, there is an article titled, "No Link Found Between Shots, Autism." In the body of the article it says, "There may be rare incidences, with a small number of children, where the MMR vaccine 'Could contribute' to development of autism." The MMR vaccine is supposed to protect us against Mumps, Measles and Rubella and are usually given before the age of 2.

Dr. Leonard G. Horowitz, author of <u>Emerging Viruses: Aids and Ebola, Nature, Accident or Intentional</u>? is very much against vaccines. He talks about what we don't know about vaccines and what is really in them.

I have in front of me an article about a Margaret Best who won after a 32-day trial. She had given her four and a half-month-old child the Pertussis (Whooping cough) vaccine and the Irish High Court found that it could cause brain damage. This child was left trapped with a mental age of two for the rest of his life.

I have another release dated 1998 titled, "Small Group Creates Big Arm Change, Religious Vaccine Exemption Available to All Troops." I remember

The Simplicity of Herbal Health

in 1994, Hanna told us that the Gulf War Vets would come home with many physical problems not related to the war, but from all the vaccines that they were required to take.

When my daughter was little, from baby to nine years old, she was a trouper. She took her vaccines and it was OK. After the age of nine, she told me that there had to be a better way to do things than inserting a needle into a body with foreign matter. She told me that it was barbaric. At the time, I didn't agree with her...as most of you don't, but I have come to understand the whole process better. What did Dr. Robert Mendelsohn say? " To be fair, Mendelsohn admits that doctors don't intentionally do things to hurt their patients. 'They really believe that infant formula is just as good as breast milk', He says ' They believe that ultrasound is no more harmful than the sound of the human voice. Doctors do things with the best intentions ...just like the priests of the inquisition.'"

I have an article dated Feb. 20, 2000 from The New-Press, Fort Meyers, Florida stating that Barbara Loe Fisher, founder of the Virginia based National Vaccine Information Center, got involved when "her son, Chris, then 2 got DTP and oral polio vaccinations. Within four hours, the toddler suffered from convulsions, shock and unconsciousness." Barbara feels that this left him with "multiple learning disabilities and attention deficit disorders."

For more reading on vaccines here are a couple of books that one can check out: <u>A Shot In The Dark</u> by Harris L. Coulter and Barbara Loe Fisher, Avery Publishing and <u>Vaccines: Are They Really Safe and Effective</u>? by Neil Z. Miller, New Atlantean Press.

Every area in the country mandates a number of vaccines before the children can be enrolled in school. I have heard that most kids by the age of 4 have had as many as 20 vaccines. I don't know if that is true, but in my area the children are required to have a Hepatitis B shots before being allowed to attend school. According to my Merck Manual, "Hepatitis B virus is less easily transmitted than Hepatitis A virus. One way it can be transmitted is through contaminated blood or blood products." Is school that violent that kindergartners might exchange blood? (Another good reason for home schooling.)

So we are back to the fact that this is a planet of choice. Choose wisely.

* * *

I would like to return to Juvenile Diabetes and talk a little more about how foreign protein gets into the body because vaccines are just one way. This protein has to be just the right weight and acceptable by the beta cells. Well, there are many ways for this to happen, one might be stepping on a nail. Or this person might have an ulcer in the stomach lining. Another way is that either parasites have drilled small holes in the intestinal walls or Candida made the holes, and by drinking homogenized milk (Homogenize -To reduce to particles and disperse throughout a fluid- American Heritage College Dictionary), we have protein going from the intestinal tract into the intestinal cavity.

O-kay, so why doesn't every child get this? It only happens if certain conditions are present. If the liver isn't functioning properly, if there is a genetic weakness in the pancreas and if the protein is the right molecular weight.

How does the medical profession handle Juvenile Diabetes? Because the immune system is destroying "self" cells that are needed, the medical profession wants to shut down the immune system to put some control on this process, and supplement with substances that these cells would normally make (insulin). This leaves the body open to every dis-ease that is going around.

As herbalists, we like to suggest Astragalus. This herb is in the category of boosting and assisting the immune system, only it works a lot different than the usual immune boosters.

We are all familiar with Echinacea as the herb of choice when we are coming down with something because we know that it will work hard to search out and get rid of the "bad guys." And it does its job beautifully.

We have also mentioned that Calendula petals do basically the same thing and that it might be prudent to do Echinacea for a while then switch to Calendula.

Now let's talk about Astragalus, the third immune booster and how this one works a differently? Astragalus works by the hour. It keeps the immune system healthy and working but it isn't in any hurry to get the job

The Simplicity of Herbal Health

done. When you take one of the other two immune boosters, they work by the job and want to do a lot quickly, but with Astragalus...well, it takes its own sweet time. It does the job of getting rid of the "not me" cells but so slowly that the body can rebuild some "me" right behind it. The best part is that it keeps the immune system running but at a slower pace.

I found something of interest in <u>An Elders Herbal</u> about this, "Pharmacology points to plant constituents such as saponins and complex polysaccharies as key components in the immunological role of herbs, but always remember that herbs act as biological wholes, not simply as vehicles for 'active ingredients'."

I was approached recently regarding a company that is selling capsules of plant sugars (monosaccharides and polysaccharides) to heal just about everything. It sounded wonderful, but I still believe in the wholesome state of the herb instead of the part-some of its components.

Astragalus will increase interferon and antibodies in the body. It helps in the elimination of toxins while supporting the liver. Dr. Ritchason states, "It supports liver and spleen function and in supporting the liver, protects it against chemical damage caused by chemotherapy and also helps to normalize blood pressure. When added to the program, Astragalus actually doubles the life of cancer patients who opted to be treated by chemotherapy and radiotherapy."

Astragalus has anti-clotting agents and assists in protecting the heart along with improving the body's circulation.

It gives energy to the body by improving the health of the adrenals. Some of the other things that it is used for is Candida, Epstein-Barr virus, Flu, Heart disease, Hepatitis, Kidneys, Ulcers, Thymus, Stress, Metabolism (raises), and has even been used successfully for night sweats.

In Dr. Duke's database I found less than 50 constituents for this herb. We are talking about *Astragalus membranaceus*. The reason that I mention the Latin name of this herb is because in the <u>National Audubon Field Guide to North American Wildflowers</u>, I found a cousin commonly named Woolly Locoweed. A member of the pea family with the Latin name of *Astragalus mollissimus* and this cousin lives in "Prairies and sandy soil. Across southwestern Canada; South Dakota and Minnesota south to Texas and beyond." The comment made by this publication is that this cousin isn't very nice as it contains toxic substances.

I read that with tongue in cheek because many medicinal plants contain properties that would not be healthy by themselves but then neither is Chemotherapy. As an example: the fruit of the apple tree contains arsenic in its seeds, but when the horse eats the wholesome apple (seeds and all), the toxins are neutralized. This is why I am an advocate of wholesome herbs and not their parts. When all the constituents are working together they are most healing.

How do herbalists work on Juvenile Diabetes? Start with a good diet of the 5 things; fruits, vegetables, whole grains, nuts and seeds. Then cut out all simple carbohydrates. I know that giving up pizza is hard but if we really work at this, the doctor will cut the insulin back and maybe some day.... Then we would add the herbal formulas that Dr. Christopher recommended: the liver formula, the lower bowel formula, the blood formula, the pancreas formula and the adrenal formula along with Astragulas. Not all at once but over time we would be cleaning this body and helping it get back to the way it was designed. This is not an easy undertaking. It might take years but the body will heal itself if given the right building blocks. Dr. Christopher said that if insulin isn't available one should take large amounts of his pancreas formula.

In a Hanna Kroeger lecture one February, while talking about diabetes, she said that one should take six long stem dandelions and cut them into a raw salad for lunch and repeat this for dinner. Do this for 12 days and "you will have no diabetes. The longer the stems, the better. Combine with anything else in the salad and cover with any dressing."

After she was done telling us this, a lady in the back of the room stood up. She wanted to know where she could get long stemmed dandelions for her son who had diabetes. Hanna told her that she should work on the parasites first and get the dandelions in the spring. She mentioned that anyone with that much sweet in their body was loaded with parasites.

Another thing that she suggested for Diabetes was to grow green beans until they bud, then cut the whole plant, cook and eat it. She mentioned that the energy goes from the roots to the leaves to the fruit.

The Simplicity of Herbal Health

According to Hanna, the pancreas represents just how you digest the sweetness in your life.

Remember that herbs are foods and can be used on an hourly basis when in a crisis.

What works with what?

Hanna had a list of foods that go together to give us energy. The list said that meats of all kinds go with vegetables of all kinds. That fruit of all kinds go with grains of all kinds. She suggested that Tea, Grapefruit, Lemons, Limes and Watermelon should be eaten by themselves if you want energy. She also said that Apples and Rice go with anything. So what is the first thing that we do? We put meat on bread and call it a sandwich. Is it any wonder that by 2:00 in the afternoon, we are running out of energy?

One of the hints in her book is that fruit is a great detoxifier. She mentions that you cannot build and detoxify at the same time.

She said that "Meat and Milk is a NO-NO" Meat needs acids like vinegar or salad dressing to start the digestion in the stomach. Milk is alkaline.

"Alkaline fruits are: Apples, Apricots, Bananas, Berries, Cherries, Citron, Currants, Grape, Grapefruit, Raisins, Tangerines, Melon, and Oranges. Alkaline Vegetables are: Almonds, Artichokes, Asparagus, Beans (dried), Beans (fresh), Beets, Beet tops, Brussels Sprouts, Cabbage, Carrot, Cauliflower, Celery, Lettuce, Mushrooms, Olives, Onions, Parsley, Parsnip, Peas (fresh), Peppers, Raw Potatoes (with peeling), Radish, Squash, Tomatoes, and Turnips. And to increase your alkalinity, use one half teaspoon baking soda in 6 ounces of water 2 times daily," according to Hanna.

My sister didn't believe that some of the things listed above were Alkaline. I brought out a book called <u>Alkalize or Die</u> by Dr. Theodore A Baroody. In this book he explains what Hanna is trying to say. He says that these foods are alkaline forming when they get into the body. It works on an electro-chemical basis where certain minerals in the food are acid-binding and leave an alkaline-formed ash in the urine.

"Acid foods are: Bran, Bread (rye), Corn, Rice, Sugar, Tapioca, Cornstarch, Grains, Molasses, Oatmeal, Pastries, Peanuts, Popcorn,

Phyllis Heitkamp Master Herbalist

Peeled Potatoes, Preserves, Spaghetti, Cheese, Clams, Crabs, Eggs, Fish, Meats, Chicken, Oysters, Turkey, Shrimp and Lentils. Increase acidity with vinegar water," again according to Hanna

She suggests that in addition to the acid/alkaline problem, all foods have vibrations and this needs to be taken into consideration.

The Simplicity of Herbal Health

Hanna's Miscellaneous Notes

Aloe Vera can be used to energize the spine. Place one piece of leaf of Aloe near the base of the spine and allow the energy to travel up the spine to the head. Don't take concentrated Aloe Vera juice.

Using the word "Aurum" will help keep America out of trouble. This is the Latin word for Gold.

Apple peel tea pulls off arsenic and promotes mental acuity. Arsenic goes to the muscles.

For Arthritis: make the body more acid and check for protozoa (single celled parasite). Eliminate wheat, rice and corn from the diet.

The Aura is the blueprint of the body.

With numbness and pain on the back, check for Norwalk Virus. It is found up and down the spine. If Norwalk is not treated, it will become Meningitis. If the problem is horizontally across the hips, check for Coxsackie Virus. When Coxsackie goes systemic, it mimics any and all diseases.

Bless food to increase its life force and negate the harmful effects of chemicals. Always bless bread that has been cut by a knife.

Compresses of Comfrey can be used to rebuild broken bones.

The loss of smell comes from cadmium poisoning.

Butter on your bread in the morning will increase your aura.

People with carbon monoxide poisoning can't wake up fresh in the morning. Carbon Monoxide changes to lead in the body. Recent studies in the LA area showed that children in that area had high lead content in their blood.

Lead poisoning can effect people differently. Women can't get out of bed and men get exhausted by 4:00 pm. Children will become hyperactive or emotionally disturbed. Lead looks like calcium to the skin and bones and it is absorbed within 2 hours.

Carpal Tunnel Syndrome comes from not feeling sufficiently appreciated. Manipulate wrist to end of fingers, starting with the outside down to the pinky. Do Each finger 12 times...up and down.

Cashew Nut Butter is a 4th dimensional product. It is good for physical and spiritual traumas.

Cauliflower or Broccoli, even in small amounts, are better for you than milk and contain more calcium.

When Chiropractic adjustments don't hold, it is always because of stress.

Silver will keep colds away. Eat off your silverware and stay healthy. Dark forces cannot get through silver. Silver is lacking in Epstein-Barr Virus. Use salt and soda to clean your silverware not the chemical cleaners that are available.

Crystals are thought enhancers. They magnify your thoughts 10 to 100%.

Use 1 ear candle in the navel to pull out emotions. Emotional trouble can escalate into leukemia.

Flowers and their colors:

Pink Tulips/lilies = Spiritual
Yellow Daylilies = Female
Clover = Cancer (Make Clover Tea)
Purple Iris = Infections
Small Carnations = Emotions
Straw Flowers = Collagen in the system
Daisy = Viral infections.

Decaffeinated coffee is a no-no as it has too many chemicals in it.

Hanna suggests for forgiveness, that you write the trauma at night and read it in the morning, then burn it. Do this until you don't have anything

The Simplicity of Herbal Health

left to write. She says that it should be gone in 7 days. She mentioned that talking about a problem just makes it bigger, writing about it, makes it smaller.

To get rid of something in the body, Hanna suggests that shouting, "Shoo, Shoo, Shoo", three times at the problem, will make it go away.

Herbs work on the earth body. Vibrationals work on the spiritual body.

Vibrationals should be taken by themselves and never mixed with each other or with herbs. When taking them, do not eat 10 minutes before taking them or 10 minutes after and refrain from using products with Peppermint in them. (Toothpaste, etc.)

For joint pain, Hanna suggests 1 quart distilled water, 6 level tablespoons of cream of tarter and 2 tablespoons of borax. Combine and add to bath water. Soak.

Legionnaire's disease is a virus with a parasite around it. Air conditioning and swamp coolers introduce it.

✷ Lemon converts to alkaline when a lot of it is used.

For Lupus, Hanna suggests checking for Protozoa (a single celled parasite).

Microwaves change the vibrations of things from plus to minus.

To eliminate mind control, she suggests that you hold your fingers on the dent in the back of the head where the spine and the skull connect.

Petunia flower tea will calm the emotions in both children and adults alike.

Pneumonia can be dealt with by placing your right hand on the person's forehead and the left hand behind the head. Hold until they take a very deep breath.

Yellows Potatoes are best, Red potatoes are good but white potatoes gobble up sprays. Cut the eyes out of the potato. This goes for another member of this family. Cut the tomato top off, where it was connected to the vine. With this on, the tomato is not good for humans.

For radio active fallout Hanna suggests using a salt and soda bath. She also suggests using willow leaf tea. Boil the leaves to make 2 gallons of tea.

Ritalin is the same as LSD. Hanna feels that when the child is taken off the prescription, they usually go to street drugs.

When the scapula is out of place, the body needs more protein.

For stuttering, Hanna suggests wrapping hands around both ankles for 3 minutes.

Tears heal the emotions.

Teflon goes to the lungs.

The Simplicity of Herbal Health

Hanna's Workbook

Hanna has a workbook that is used to find out what the situation is that needs to be handled. She believes that there are <u>Seven Physical and Seven Spiritual Causes of Ill Health.</u>

The Physical Causes are: Neglect, Trauma, Congestion, Environmental toxins, Parasites, Infections, and Miasma.

The Spiritual Causes are: Neglect, Trauma, Congestion, Karma, Dark Forces, Emotions, and Law of the Universe.

Under each of these categories, she has from one to thirty things that could be causing the problem.

She suggests using Kinesiology (muscle testing) or the Pendulum (Dowsing) to find out exactly which cause to work on.

While I was studying at the School of Natural Healing in Utah, they gave a class on iridology (The studies of the iris of the eye as a way to understand what the problems in the body are, based on the spots or lines in the iris of the eyes.) As I was already proficient with a pendulum, I preferred to continue using that system.

Hanna found that a lot of people have trouble dealing with a pendulum. Not the using of it but the fact of it. They associate it with witchcraft or the devil or some such thing. It is not that at all. She wrote a book called *The Pendulum, The Bible and Your Survival* in 1973. In it she talks about the fact that many biblical leaders used a rod to get answers that would help their nomadic tribes. If they were to go left over those hills, would they find grass for their animals or would someone have been there before them? A lot of nomadic animals have a tendency to take the grasses down to the roots and the recovery time is not short, even near water.

Some people ask me if herbalism is New Age? None of this is NEW. In Psalms, David spoke of needing both a rod and a staff. Aaron and Moses carried a "Rod". My Grandfather used a "rod" to find artesian wells. Herbs have always been used.

Phyllis Heitkamp Master Herbalist

To use a pendulum, one holds it with three fingers, the index finger (Positive), the middle finger (Negative) and the thumb (Neutral). Holding the pendulum over the index finger of the other hand, one asks to be shown a positive indicator. "Show me my 'yes'." Then doing this again over the middle finger of the hand that is not holding the pendulum, one asks to be shown a "no". Why do we do this, because we are all different. My "yes" is a circle, where my "no" is no movement at all (a plumb line, if you will.) I have a friend whose "yes" is a clockwise circle and her "no" is a counter-clockwise circle.

Hanna made us practice until we could do it well because she told us that we need to be responsible for our own lives. We need to access information that we have no knowledge of, but that God does. We need to access more of what is available to us. We have become very dependent people. Tell me what is wrong with me. Tell me if you think I should .... In biblical days, people got answers from God but now it is only a one way street. We just ask and hope that we are doing what He wants us to do. We ask, "Should I move?" And if we don't happen to have a new location pop into our view, we decide that the answer must have been "no" or else something would have miraculously shown up. But no one thinks that miracles are new age.

Even Einstein talked about the need to access more "of our brain power." I took a class in California where they talked about the fact that all the information is out there, we just need to fine tune ourselves to access it. They equated it to a radio and we need to tune in.

Using a pendulum, one can find water and ask how deep it is or is it worth digging a well here.

We live in an information age where incoming information is overwhelming. Here we can use a pendulum with books to check out which chapter to read to get the essence of that book instead of grinding through 300 pages.

We can put it over a map and ask "Where does God want me to be?" Hanna said that we are always within 300 yards of help. This could be in a blizzard and the help could be just a log to crawl under until one can see again.

Using her workbook, we can check to see what vitamins and minerals are needed or what herbs would handle...something like hives in a better manner for this body. There are many herbs that do the same thing but some are more compatible for one reason or another.

More miscellaneous information

Hanna told us that we could also use personal protection in the form of our vibrations. By brushing a hand over a book, picture, check or anything that you wish to protect, no one can influence it (Change it, damage it, steal it, etc.).

She also had a "lazer" light that was constructed to assist the body in increasing energy to the parathyroid. This Lazer could be used for many other things such as cleaning the vibrations on the outside of a body but it could also be used to clear dark forces from an area. She mentioned that by making the sign of the cross on a wall with the lazer light and speaking, "In the name of God, I clear this room of all dark forces", one could clean out the negative forces from a room. This is to be done on all six surfaces of that room.

She believed that even though we live in the 21st century, there are dark forces that abound. She told us that the "Logos" (Word) was very strong. We, who live in a body on this planet, are stronger than the negative energies around us. By using our words wisely, we can make changes. Most of us feel that we are powerless in this world, but we have the backing of a powerful God.

This is not a religious book but an herbal book. The only reason that this information is in here is because a lot of our problems are on the Spiritual side. There is no one that does exorcisms in today's world. Hanna shows us how to do this and in "casting out demons" we are healing. Check out her book called, The Seven Spiritual Causes of Ill Health reprinted in 1997. (ISBN 1-882713-00-5)

I have "bumped" into negative forces causing ill health a lot and have been chastised for knowing this. I even had a minister call me to tell me that none of his people have "negative forces" in or around them. Then why were they sick?

Phyllis Heitkamp Master Herbalist

Hanna suggested typing the 91st Psalm in very small print and in a narrow, perpendicular line. Then cutting this strip, rolling it up and placing this Psalm, with a thumb tack, over the entrance to your dwelling as a way to keep negative forces out. I have this and a small pouch of Indian tobacco tacked behind my front door. No one notices it but I know that it is there. This way the negative energy that people carry around is left outside my dwelling.

I called Hanna once to ask her about Salt. She had a map of the United States and had a lot of herbs and stones and salt on it. I wanted to know if salt would draw moisture to it or repel it. I didn't want to flood an area of my US map this way. She told me in her very broken English, "Oh, no my dear, Salt repels the dark forces." I have since put rock salt in small vials and have them in all four corners of my home. If you intend to do this, do a cleansing of the house first with Hyssop or Sage.

Other Healing Modalities

Bach Flower Remedies

There are so many other healing modalities that are available, one of which is Bach Flower Remedies. Dr. Bach realized that each plant has abilities to heal our bodies. If this is true, then each flower containing all of these abilities is ready to pass them on to future generations of that particular plant.

Throughout this book we have talked about vibrationals and Bach knew that these vibrations influence not only the body but also the area around our bodies. We are not just physical bodies. I used the term "meat bodies" once and really upset a lady that I was talking to. We have a spiritual body, an emotional body, a mental body, and a physical body all in this space. I kind of liked what I heard a long time ago from a speaker on this subject when he said, "What if my body is just a sliver in my soul?"

Dr. Bach knew that some of the healing of herbs comes from the vibrations that they emit and if the herb does this, then perhaps the flowers do this also. He did a system of tests and found out what vibrations acted on what areas of the body or situation and has catalogued these for healing.

When my Mom had a stroke, I arrived in the emergency room to find her not able to talk but wide-eyed and very frightened. I carry Bach's Rescue Remedy in my purse and although she could not swallow, I placed it on her lips. I could see her calming down.

I had my own experience with Rescue Remedy. While rollerblading with my daughter, I hit a twig and fell, breaking my wrist. We went to the emergency room and while waiting to get it X-rayed, I could feel my body going into shock. I instructed my daughter to give me some Rescue Remedy orally. I could feel stability returning. As in every emergency room, we waited for a very long time, so I asked my daughter to give me a little more and she kidded me about it, "Hey Mom, do you want me to pour it down you?" We had a good laugh but it really does work.

Vibrational remedies like Bach's work very well on animals. I have a friend who works with horses and she told me that when she gives a remedy to a horse, they don't question it but prance off. In a little while they shake their whole body and come back to her. When she checks them out, she finds that the situation has corrected itself.

You can make your own flower remedies by removing the flower from the plant with tweezers, (We only want the vibration of the flower, not from our fingers) and place it in a glass bowl that is half-full of distilled water. This is covered with cheesecloth to keep the bugs out and placed in the sun for 6 to 8 hours. The vibration of the flower is transferred to the water. After hours in sunshine, the flower is removed with tweezers. The water is then infused with a bit of vinegar to preserve it and it is placed in dark bottles and labeled for later use.

Aromatherapy

Another healing method is through the plant's aromatic oils. The oils in some plants disperse and give off a wonderful and sometimes not-so wonderful smell.

This type of healing takes place through our olfactory nerve. These nerves are present in the nose and sinus areas.

I have used this for many things and found that the oils can heal buildings too. When our neighborhood was flooded, 2 inches of water came up in from our drain in the basement floor before we were able to plug it. We bailed the water and vacuumed the remaining out, but the carpeting in the basement was still wet. I talked to my friend, Karen, who is an aromatherapist, among other things, and she suggested that I use a diffuser with Tea Tree Oil in it to eliminate any fungus that wants to set up housekeeping in my carpeting. This done, we never had a problem with future odors or any sign of fungus.

Oils are concentrated herbs. It takes 50 pounds of plant matter to get one-half ounce of plant oil. A lady came to me that was taking an oil combination internally but was having a problem. It seemed that parasites were crawling out of the pores of her skin. I explained to her that oils need to be "thinned" with carrier oils because they are so potent. With this much toxicity, they were much too strong for her to take the way she was doing it.

Oils work well because they are herbs in concentration.

Because of the oils in herbs and how very healing they are to the body, it is imperative that all herbal containers remain covered when not in use, otherwise half of the healing properties will be lost to the air.

Reflexology

Here we have another wonderful healing modality. Doctor Christopher used this many times on people's feet. When he gave someone an herbal combination to move stones in the kidneys or when the colon was blocked, he worked on the bottoms of the feet to help stimulate these organs. The premise is that, on the bottoms of the feet as well as on the hands and the head, there are nerve endings that connect with the different organs or body parts and by stimulating these nerve endings, one can activate that area of the body.

The School of Natural Healing sometimes called it "Zone Therapy."

I have been told that there are three points to this healing modality. One is that it releases and relaxes or reduces the tension and congestion in the body. The second is that it improves circulation and lastly, it helps to normalize body functions.

Reiki

This word is an oriental word meaning the "laying on of hands." This energy healing uses the vibrations of our bodies. We are electro-magnetic beings. As in all things electrical, the flow of energy moves from one area to another. We are not just giving away energy but flowing it through another body and back again.

We live in a world that is fighting for energy sources and the fact is that there is more than enough energy all around us.

Hydrotherapy

Doctors Post and Kellogg used this for their clients at their sanitariums in Michigan. According to Jethro Kloss, " Hydrotherapy (Water treatment) is not a cure-all. But there is no single drug on the market that can rival water in the great variety of physiological effects it is capable of producing, is wide availability, lack of bad after effects, and relative economy."

Jethro Kloss, along with his wife, operated a branch of the Battle Creek Sanitarium owned by Dr. Kellogg. Hydrotherapy was a specialty. Having water sprayed on the body to relax it or soaking in a whirlpool bath was great for the nerves and many other things. Well, all of us stay in the shower longer than necessary, sometimes just for the therapeutic value of it.

Yoga

A Hindu discipline aimed at training the consciousness for a state of perfect spiritual insight and tranquillity. As it is presently used in the United States, it is a system of exercises practiced as part of this discipline to promote control of the body and mind.

Again we are attempting to relieve the tensions. Have we found the cure-all? If we just got rid of all the tension around us, would we be well?

Visualization

Imagine it to be true and you can make it so. You are the creator of your world. What you think and do today shapes your future.

Dr. Bernard Segel, a noted cancer specialist, talked about how he used this with his patients. He liked what the children did. He had them draw a picture of their cancer and how it was being cured. Some of these children painted their cancer as black blobs and chemo as stick people with stretchers between them carrying the black blobs away.

Dr. Segel mentioned that these children were able to speed up their therapy in this manner.

Acupressure

This is much like Reflexology with the difference being that it is used all over the body and it follows the Chinese energy meridians. This is for people who would rather not do Acupuncture with needles put into the body.

Energy Healing

With this method, we are back to the basics. I have a friend who works in this area and can find energy blocks in the body. She has been trained to do this. When the energy is not flowing through our bodies, we have the on-set of dis-ease.

My daughter has had skin problems of various kinds for many years. Nothing that we have tried has handled it. Then I heard about something that Dr. Wayne Dyer was using for his family to keep them in optimum health. It has to do with energy. By sending a picture of yourself to this place, it is analyzed and the energy problem is identified. This picture is then put into a machine where the correcting vibration is projected to the body owning the picture.

We are known by our vibrations. Just as each thing around you is vibrating in a different pattern, so are bodies. Hanna said that we could use a picture of a person, taken since their last blood transfusion or organ transplant. (These things change our vibration) If they have never had either, we can use a picture of them when they were 3 years old or in kindergarten.

Other Healing Methods

There are many more avenues to healing the body, mind and spirit. I could never include all of them here. There are many healers alive today and one of them is the person who is reading this material. You are the healer of your body. How you do this is up to you.

Phyllis Heitkamp Master Herbalist

Herbal Health

We are living on planet Earth and have been given everything that we need to have life abundant.

In this book I have tried to show, the "what" and the "how" to do this. Most books that I have read tell what to use for this or that. Hanna did a lot of that but I wanted to know how to use it. I want the reader to know that they can use a single herb and make it into any form that is described in this book.

There are books such as <u>A Modern Herbal,</u> by Mrs. Grieve, that tells us what part of the plant to use but I still wanted to know what to do with these plant parts. After my students learn how to make medicines, I still have them call me to jog their memories on how to make this or that.

It is pleasing to me to see as many people as there are that are willing to experiment and try things, because when they do and they find that it really works the way they were taught, they start to use herbs more and more. Then they start to listen to their bodies and start taking responsibility for their health.

I wrote to a gardener that had written a book. I told her how I had experimented with some of her suggestions and really liked them. The reply that I received was that a lot of people read all the material but then never use it or even try. She said that we are so educated toward reading and wanting the information but so afraid to try for fear we will not do it just right. We have been trained to fear failure but it is in failure that we learn the most. When something turns out right, we forget about it because we expected it to be that way but when it turns out wrong, we have to figure out how to make it right. As a student, we choose A over B and it if was correct, we never thought about the question or the answer again.

I like people to use what they have available. The things that are growing around them are for their health. Learning to use it to stay or get healthy is what this book is all about. With the help of this book, and following a life style that is in conjunction with these principles, one should live a comfortable life. Perhaps along the way, we might be able to assist others in this endeavor.

Survival is helping others, not competing in the game of life.

By eating correctly, drinking good water, getting exercise and rest, along with keeping a positive attitude, we will remain in good health.

Chapter VI – Resources

Baroody, Theodore A., ND, DC, CNC, *Alkalize or Die,* Holographic Health Press, Waynesville, NC., 1991, 241 pg.

Duke, James A., Ph.D., *Dr. Duke's Phytochemical and Ethnobotanical Database,* 2003

Foster, Steven, *Herbal Renaissance,* Gibb Smith, Layton, UT, 1984, 234 pg.

Hoffmann, David, M.N.I M.H., *An Elders' Herbal,* Healing Arts Press, Rochester, VT., 1993, 266 pg.

Reprinted with permission from *Back To Eden* by Jethro Kloss, Lotus Press, PO Box 325, Twin Lakes, WI. 53181. © 1999 All Rights Reserved.

Kroeger, Hanna, *Cookbook for Electro-Chemical Energies,* 1986

Kroeger, Hanna, Ms.D, *Good Health Through Special Diets,* Hanna Kroeger Publications, Boulder, CO, 1981

National Audubon Society Field Guide to North American Wildflowers, Niering, Wm. A. Botany professor, Connecticut College and Olmstead, Nancy C. , Research Associate. Alfred A. Knopf, New York, NY, 1995, 269 pg.

From *The Merck Manual of Medical Information – Home Edition,* p. 1509, edited by Mark H. Beers and Robert Berkow. Copyright 1997 by Merck & Co., Inc.,Whitehouse Station, NJ.

Ritchason, Jack N.D., *The Little Herb Encyclopedia,*Woodland Health Books, Pleasant Grove, UT, 1995, 402 pg.

Simons, Lee, *Confessions of a Medical Heretic:An Interview With Dr. Robert Mendelsohn.,* Paper put out by the Vaccine Research, P.O. 4182, Northbrook, IL. 60065

Index

A

A.D.D. 89
Abscesses 46, 146
Acne 46, 117, 128, 156
Alfalfa 5, 94, 115, 172
Allergies 46
Almonds 185
Aluminum 87, 90
Amino acid 73
Angelica 51, 60
Antiaging 84
Antibiotics 133
AntiHIV 86
Antiviral 86, 126
Apple 15, 17, 28, 54, 56, 61, 68, 81, 101, 146, 164, 177, 187
Apricots 42, 68, 185
Arthritis 40, 48, 76, 187
Ascaris 21
Asparagus 11, 22, 142, 175, 185
Aspartame 78, 79, 176, 177
Asthma 46, 128, 146
Astragalus 72, 142, 182, 183

B

Bananas 142, 185
Barberry 28, 35, 36, 142
Barley 56, 94, 174
Basil 2, 50, 89, 115, 116
Bayberry 58
Beta-Blocker 80
Beta-carotene 66
BF&C 141, 144
Black Berries 59
Black Cherries 59
Black Cohosh 36, 72, 138, 142, 143, 160, 162, 163, 167, 168, 177
Black Pepper 22
Black Radish 42
Black tea 165, 171
Black Walnut 12, 17, 22, 45, 61, 113, 114, 156, 167

Bladder 36, 143, 146, 168, 179
Blood 41, 48, 76, 77, 80, 81, 117, 178, 179
Blood pressure 81
Blueberries 59
Blue Malva 69, 141, 159
Boils 46
Bowels 24
Brain 84, 85, 87
Broccoli 70, 175, 188
Bronchitis 128, 146
Burdock 46, 48, 138, 163, 172, 174
Burns 46, 117, 128
Bursitis 46
Butternut 28

C

Cadmium 74
Calamus 51, 52
Calcium 12, 36, 37, 44, 54, 68, 78, 81, 85, 86, 90, 115, 123, 144, 161, 164, 175
Cancer 15, 46, 66, 73, 117, 126, 188
Candida 19, 61, 86, 122, 126, 162, 165, 182, 183
Canker sores 20, 46
Capsicum 58, 67, 137, 146
Carbohydrates 175
Carrot 39, 160, 185
Cascara Sagrada 36
Cashews 22
Cataracts 60
Cathartic 27
Catnip 2, 15, 20, 36, 143
Cayenne 16, 17, 26, 53, 58, 67, 72, 167, 177, 179
Cervicitis 84
Chaparral 12, 17, 41, 48, 49, 74, 142, 156, 172
Chia 88
Chickenpox 117
Chickweed 59, 67, 95, 142, 146, 147, 151, 156, 161

203

Chokecherries 59
Cholesterol 37, 51, 74
Chromium 12, 32, 68, 75,
    78, 90, 173, 174
Cinnamon 18, 72
Cloves 72, 119
Coconut 52, 153
Coffee 22, 89, 161, 166
Colds 20, 146
Colic 146
Collagen 188
Colon 23, 76
Comfrey 54, 55, 81, 106, 142,
    151, 154, 156, 187
Condurango 41, 50, 74
Congestion 15, 128, 191
Constipation 76, 119, 128, 146
Copper 32, 85
Coughs 15, 46, 128
Coxsackie 50, 72, 187
Cramps 146
Cramp bark 67
Cryptomycosis 86
Cucumbers 175

D

Dandelion 16, 42, 53, 85, 94, 97,
    98, 142, 161, 163, 175
Dandruff 146
Decoction 46
Diabetics 174, 177
Diarrhea 15, 128, 146
Dill 11, 22, 168
Dioxin 21
Dyslexia 59, 89

E

Earache 21, 146
Ears 58
Echinacea 13, 44, 113, 117, 157, 182
Eczema 46
Elecampane 72
Equisetum 75
Essiac 48, 51

Estrogen 162
Eucalyptus 50, 163
Eustachian 61
Eye 59
Eyebright 58

F

Fatigue 20
FDA 12, 48, 79, 92, 122, 123
Fennel 15, 20, 35, 36, 39,
    51, 60, 160, 163
Fevers 46
Fiber 78
Flu 146, 159, 183
Fluke 21
Fluoride 44
Fomentation 35
Formula 36, 38, 41, 44, 54, 58, 59,
    60, 93, 118, 141, 143, 144, 148,
    164, 167, 168, 177, 178, 179
Foxglove 72
Fungal 21
Fungicides 86

G

Gallstones 146
Gangrene 128
Garlic 17, 36, 38, 53, 60, 72, 118,
    119, 120, 124, 167, 177
Gas 146
Gentian 36, 51
Ginger 15, 20, 26, 31, 32, 36,
    53, 72, 104, 143, 160,
    167, 168, 175, 179
Ginkgo 72, 86, 87, 88, 94
Ginseng 11, 53, 69, 72, 120,
    121, 163, 167, 177, 179
Goldenseal 17, 20, 21, 36, 38, 42,
    58, 122, 156, 167, 177
Gotu Kola 84, 88, 94, 172
Gout 46, 85
Grape 16, 36, 94, 185
Green Peppers 70
Gymnema 77

H

Hawthorn 67, 68, 69, 70, 71, 73, 75, 76, 179
Headaches 78
Heart 67, 71, 128, 183
Heartworm 21, 82
Hepatitis 40, 41, 42, 51, 153, 181, 183
Hernia 128
Herpes 46, 72, 123, 153
High blood pressure 80
Hoarseness 46
Hookworm 21
Hops 93, 94, 163
Horsetail 54, 81, 122, 123, 142, 164
Hydrophobia 91
Hyssop 2, 194

I

Impetigo 46
Iridology 59
Iron 85, 172, 175

J

Jasmine 50
Jaundice 49
Jurassic Green 94

K

Kelp 45, 161
Kidneys 26, 137, 138, 139, 168, 183

L

Lavender 2
Laxative 178
Lemon Balm 72, 123, 124
Leprosy 84
Leukemia 49
Licorice 27, 39, 40, 41, 72, 76, 156, 162, 163, 167, 177, 179
Linden 60
Liver 26, 33, 34, 36, 46, 49, 51, 54, 55, 68, 179

Lobelia 43, 44, 45, 54, 81, 92, 94, 124, 143, 156, 168, 179
Lungs 46
Lycopene 73, 96
Lymph 43, 50, 56, 128

M

Magnesium 32, 36, 68, 78, 85, 90, 115
Mandrake 28
Manganese 32, 85, 90
Maple 60, 104
Marjoram 2
Marshmallow 20, 138, 139, 140, 141, 142, 143, 148, 157, 168, 177
Measles 46, 153, 180
Melissa 64, 72, 123, 124
Menopause 162, 167
Miasma 67, 155, 191
Milk Thistle 36, 37, 156
Molasses 27, 76, 77, 83, 165, 172, 185
Mononucleosis 50, 153
Motherwort 2, 67, 71, 72
Mountain Flax 28
Mountain Grape 36
Mucusless 7, 64, 179
Mullein 43, 44, 45, 61, 94, 124, 125, 144, 156, 159, 172, 177, 179
Mushroom 166

N

Nausea 15, 128
Nerve 59, 60, 93
Nervines 90, 91, 95
Nettle 26, 135, 136, 142, 144, 163, 171, 174
Niacine 90
Nutmeg 72

O

Oak 5, 11, 12, 46, 101, 104, 107, 135, 144
Okra 22, 52, 137, 175
Olive 52, 55, 56, 151, 152, 153

Onions 70, 120, 175, 177, 185
Oregano 2, 159

P

Pancreas 41, 77, 172, 177, 178, 179
Panic attacks 86
Papilloma 50, 159, 160, 169
Paprika 41, 74
Parasites 21, 30, 49, 82, 95, 191
Parsley 53, 137, 138, 143, 168, 185
Peppermint 1, 2, 3, 26, 36, 51, 55, 72, 88, 126, 137, 142, 175, 189
Phosphorus 78, 85, 115, 175
Pineapple 22
PMS 16, 33, 162
Pneumonia 21, 189
Poison Ivy 46, 128, 135, 144
Potassium 68, 85, 114, 115, 175
Potatoes 165, 175, 185, 186, 189
Primrose 52, 117, 118, 154
Psoriasis 46, 156
Purslane 52, 154

Q

Quince 68

R

Rashes 46
Raspberry 50, 58, 97, 142, 162, 163, 167, 177
Red Clover 41, 42, 48, 66, 74, 156, 163, 172
Retrovirus 50, 51
Rose 68
Rosehips 13
Rosemary 11, 13, 60, 85, 86, 88, 160

S

Safflower 69
Sage 2, 72, 88, 126, 127, 163, 194
Salmonella 17, 18, 122, 126
Salve 151, 157
Sassafras 11, 61, 72, 82, 142

Scarlet Fever 46
Sciatica 46
Scullcap 72, 91, 94
Selenium 32, 68, 75, 90
Sesame 52, 88, 142
Shigella 18, 122
Shingles ix, x, 84, 94, 146
Single-cell 89
Sinusitis 21
Skin 46, 48, 76, 128, 144, 151
Slippery Elm 16, 20, 40, 76, 127, 128, 129, 140, 143, 147, 148, 149
Smallpox 46
Snakebite 46
Soy 53, 142, 166
Spikenard 41, 74
Stevia 77, 78, 164, 174, 176, 177
Sties 21
Strokes 76
Sucanut 76, 164
Sugars 76, 165
Sunflower 53, 161
Swelling 46, 128

T

Tapeworm 21
Tarragon 22, 50
Taurine 75
Tea Tree 82, 196
Teeth 10
Thyme 2, 13, 159
Thymus 44, 183
Thyroid 124
Tinnitus 21, 60, 61
Tomatoes 70, 165, 175, 185
Tonic 70, 178
Tonsillitis 46
Toxocara 21
Trichinosis 21
Triglycerides 37
Tuberculosis 84, 128, 155
Turkey Rhubarb 28
Typhoid 128

U

Ulcers 76, 128, 183
Uterine 76

V

Vaginitis 21, 84
Valerian 72, 90, 91, 94
Vervain 72, 159
Vinegar 15, 54, 61, 81, 118,
    146, 164, 166
Viral 21, 188
Vitamin 36, 52, 68, 70, 74, 75, 78,
    81, 95, 115, 164, 173, 175

W

Wahoo 28
Walnut 22, 28, 45, 114
Water retention 38, 46, 162
Whipworm 21
Wild Yam 35, 36, 163
Witch Hazel 158
Wood Betony 72, 92, 116, 142
Wormwood 22, 82
Wounds 21, 128

Y

Yarrow 22, 26, 51, 102, 130, 142, 162
Yeast 21, 165, 166
Yellow dock 41

Z

Zinc 11, 12, 32, 36, 78, 85

About The Author

Phyllis Heitkamp, M.H. studied with Rev. Hanna Kroeger, nationally recognized herbalist of Boulder Colorado. She received her master's degree from the School of Natural Healing of Utah, directed by David Christopher, son of Dr. John R. Christopher who founded the school. Two other teachers who have contributed to her knowledge are David Slater of Boulder Colorado and Dr. James Duke of Fulton, Maryland. The latter is retired from the U.S. Department of Agriculture as a botanist and presently author of many publications.

Phyllis works out of her home where she teaches herbal study and preparation classes along with giving lectures at Libraries, Health food stores and Book stores, Garden clubs and Churches in the State of Wisconsin She also schedules educational herbal walks. The latest series of classes being given at Kaukauna's 1000 Island Nature Preserve.

For the past couple of years, she has been on the board of directors for Wellspring of Newburg, which is an organic farm/Bed and Breakfast/ educational retreat.

She has taught classes at LaFarge Adult Education, lectured at Cardinal Stritch College, appeared on the live television program called *Mastering The Presents* featured on Warner Cable, and been a guest on a radio program sponsored by Sunseed Natural Foods of West Bend.

Her book *Wisconsin Medicinal Herbs* was published in 1999 and is distributed throughout the state of Wisconsin. She has written articles for a few publications including, *the Gate* – Green Bay, *New Avenues* – Janesville and *The Scoop* – Grafton, and is listed on *The Healers* websight, (*www.thehealers.org/index.html*) having written articles for them in the past.

Her goal is to continue learning about the healing properties in herbs and be able to disseminate this information to interested parties. To continue this goal, she is at oakwelherb@aol.com for comments. To keep abreast of new healing methods as they appear and new ideas in this field. To help other's reduce their use of chemicals by making informed decisions. The Internet has provided a way to keep past students informed of new information as it surfaces.

I cannot teach anyone anything.
I can only make them think.
Socrates

615.321 H36s
Heitkamp, Phyllis.
The simplicity of herbal
health : FEB 1 5 2005

Some underlining

Printed in the United States
22062LVS00004B/118-207

9 781418 422509